Sta

Stay

Four Pillars for Living Life and Finishing Well

Jim McGuire

Contents

Acknowledgments

To Alison Syring, developmental editor: Thank you for your persistence, patience, and above all, professionalism in bringing this book to completion. Your kindness and encouragement throughout the process made this an enjoyable adventure.

To Kim: Thank you for sharing life together. I marvel at your ability to excel at whatever you set your mind to do. I have been the beneficiary of your profound generosity and commitment to excellence.

To Kaylee, Joel, and Jonathan: You captured my heart and taught me more than you will ever know.

To all who have influenced my life through your love and friendship. To each, I am forever grateful.

Preface

In my nineteen years as a hospice chaplain, I have had the distinct privilege of providing pastoral care to more than four thousand individuals and their families. I have traveled to almost every town and village within forty miles of my office. There is hardly a neighborhood where I have not visited someone in their home, nursing home or hospital, and in many neighborhoods I have visited several homes. I have been at this long enough that I now visit the next generation of the same family. The numbers are staggering. In addition, I have officiated at hundreds of funeral and memorial services.

For several years, my wife, Kim, has prompted me to consider this rich work experience that I have enjoyed. She reminds me that my work is unique among the job force and that others could benefit from what I have learned. Our daughter, Kaylee, and her friend, Becky, often prod me to, "Tell us a hospice story, Dad." Even into their adult years, they continue to ask for a story of someone I served under hospice care. My response remains, "There are so many unique stories that not one stands out as remarkable." But the truth is, like each birth, each death is unique and bears telling. There is a lesson to be learned with each passing, if we are willing to learn. And so I decided to write this book, with a few reasons in mind.

First, those finishing their earthly journeys are an often-underutilized perspective for those of us still living ours. They provide a perspective on life, relationships, and what is truly valuable. The dying person sees life as it truly is: a brief pilgrimage that passes too quickly. We can, if we so choose, better understand our existence if we occasionally remind ourselves of the reality of its brevity. The dying experience this reality daily. For many of them, they see the complexity of this world in its simplest form. We can learn from this seldom-tapped resource—if we are willing to come under their tutelage.

Second, I wrote this book as a reminder that humans long for connection. It is hardwired into our biology. From our very beginning, we are all living as a result of conception, nurture, and birth. We experience many of life's pleasures when in the company of others. Yet, for some, relationships are stress-filled, difficult, and painful. The stories of individuals who have succumbed to their disease progression are hallowed examples of life lived in the company of others. Most are shining examples for us to emulate. I have written of human connection with the hope that the reader will contemplate their own life's connections.

Third, I have written this book as my way of honoring the many individuals who welcomed me, a stranger, into the sacred space called dying. While their voices are now still, they remain a constant reminder of the sanctity of every human life. We value their lives and their stories and value their contribution to the world we inhabit. Their stories, to some degree, are a part of our stories, and our stories will be part of the stories of those who follow us. By telling their stories, we pay tribute to their lives.

Finally, I owe a great debt of gratitude to the many coworkers who value my ministry service and honor my role on the hospice team.

In the course of our lives, we meet countless individuals who pass us by if it be but for a moment; others are with us for a lifetime. Each one has a purpose. I have the distinct privilege to be on stage with people as their curtain closes for the last time. The final scene of a person's earthly life never disappoints. Like a good play, it always leaves the audience with something to contemplate. May this story leave you with something to contemplate as well.

Introduction

Like a good recipe, a good book is as much about what you leave out as what you put in. As I began the process of writing this book, four lessons on life, work, and relationships emerged. These four pillars are foundational for building a life that will provide greater personal satisfaction and help one withstand the challenges of life. They are lessons that I have learned through my nineteen years as a hospice chaplain. Additionally, I was often able to observe these four pillars as the personal traits of many of the individuals who navigated the dying process with the greatest sense of clarity and purpose. This attitude not only benefited them, but also promoted a greater acceptance among their family members and friends.

The four pillars I have identified are: Stay Focused, Stay Calm, Stay Humble, and Stay True to Yourself. Critical to the success of these four pillars is the word stay. You see, it's not only important that we practice these behaviors, but it's also important that each becomes an intricate part of our lives. Without exception, the people whom I encounter and who embody these pillars tend to experience a more enjoyable and satisfying life—and death.

But let me pause for a moment on that word, death. In the early stages of writing this book, it occurred to both my wife, Kim, and I that overuse of words like death, dying, and die created a morbid, almost depressing tone. This was not my intent when I began formulating my thoughts for the book, nor is it my goal as I work with those who are dying. Occasionally someone will ask me, "How do you work with dying people all day long and for all these years?" My answer has not changed since I started this work on October 1, 2000, and it has not changed as I wrote this book: "I focus on the living."

As you will discover in reading this book, the person with the terminal diagnosis is always my primary focus. But when I am with them, I do not focus on their dying; rather, I focus on helping them live in the present moment. I focus on helping them live the best possible life for as long as they live. I do not define for them what makes for the best possible life; rather, they define this for me. After all, it's their life. I know they are dying, they know they are dying, so unless they ask me what they should expect in their final days, the conversation does not always lead there. I do encourage the person to take care of as much as possible while they still have the physical and mental ability. Later in the book, I will address why this is so important.

So how does the reader experience the greatest personal benefit from this book? It depends upon what you, the reader, need. The book is written with you in mind, and as such, I hope that each person can use it in the way they see fit. One can read each chapter individually, reflect, and practice that behavior. Or the book can be read for small group discussion. Following each chapter, there are thought-provoking questions designed to encourage self-assessment and group interaction. Of course, the book can be read for personal enjoyment and edification, too, as one reads memoirs detailing my life's work among those finishing their earthly lives.

Throughout the book, I use anecdotal stories of people I have met in my work. Their names and any identifiable information have been changed in order to honor their privacy and comply with HIPPA law. Any similarities to known persons are coincidental and attest more to the commonality of the human experience. The stories are identifiable because they represent each of our stories. This is a key reason why I wrote the book. We can learn so much about life from one another. But the lessons we can learn about life by those finishing theirs is beyond measure. Here is to a life well lived.

Chapter One: Stay Focused

On May 25, 1961, President John F. Kennedy boldly declared: "I believe that this Nation should commit itself to achieving the goal, before this decade is out, of landing a man on the moon and returning him safely to earth." On July 24, 1969, our nation accomplished that goal when Apollo 11 returned safely to earth. There is little doubt that this mission would have been completed, if not for sustained focus.

The Lewis and Clark Expedition (1804-1806) was considered a success because it accomplished a number of its stated goals, including discovering a westward route across the continent, conducting research, and establishing relationships with indigenous people. Their sustained focus helped pave the way for a burgeoning nation.

Marie Currie (1867-1934), physicist and chemist, spent years in focused research. Her findings still influence the medical and energy sectors of our society. Countless lives have been improved and extended because of her discoveries. It is this type of sustained focus that has allowed humankind to engineer many of life's advancements.

What do these three examples have in common? There is little doubt that we would have put a man on the moon, mapped a westward route across a continent, or made scientific advancements without sustained focus on the purpose of each mission. Focus is important for humankind to move forward in big ways, but focus is important in small ways, too.

As a chaplain, whenever I visit a person, I pay careful attention to the environment into which I am entering. Even before I enter a person's home, I am assessing the immediate surroundings. Do they live in a rural setting or urban neighborhood? People tend to live in locations that reflect their personality, so these early details can give me clues about the person I am going to meet.

Our particular hospice agency serves a large geographical area, which has both urban and rural communities. Generally, there is a different mindset between those who live in an urban environment and those who live in the rural countryside. Rural dwellers like space between themselves and their neighbors. They tend to place a premium on their privacy. Urban dwellers tend to be more comfortable in confined settings. They may not always welcome a neighbor's input or friendly gesture, but they recognize the community in which they live. Sounds from an adjacent apartment or nearby neighbor are commonplace in an urban environment.

When I drive into a person's neighborhood, I stay focused on whether it is a new subdivision or an older established area. If it is a new subdivision, chances are the terminal diagnosis was either recently given or unexpected. Why do I come to this conclusion? Humans tend to become more cautious, not less, after receiving such devastating news. Buying a house in a new subdivision is usually something people do when they think that they have a long time to enjoy the home, not when they are nearing the end of their life. At the same time, there are occasions when a dying spouse will move into a new living space such as a condominium, townhouse, or apartment. This move is usually in preparation for their loved one's benefit. The new living situation will better serve the needs of the surviving family member when the patient passes.

In addition to paying attention to a person's neighborhood, we can become even more nuanced in our focus by looking at the details that surround a person. Let me explain.

When making a visit, I look for clues that may help me understand this person's priorities. For instance, what does the outside of the house tell me about the person? Are there cutesy yard monuments, a "Welcome to Grandma and Grandpa's Place" sign, a painted birdhouse on the front porch, or a pull along camper in the back of the house? I look for clues about a person wherever I can find them. Are they new to the nursing home or have they lived there for several years? Is this a recent diagnosis or have they been dealing with this illness for a long time? I do my due diligence before I meet the person whenever possible, and I pay attention, as these answers help me focus on the individual during our interaction.

Stay

When I finally arrive at a person's home, nursing home, or hospital room, I must stay focused on the purpose of my visit. The visit must be patient-focused, or patient-centric. The patient's needs must remain the top priority. The visit is never about my needs; rather, it is about the patient's needs. They, not I, set the agenda for the visit. The conversation goes wherever they want it to go. In fact, there is only conversation if they want it. Trying to force a conversation with someone does not help the person. I may get my voice heard, but how has that person been served?

While it is important for me to pay attention to the details that clue me into the person I am meeting, this attention to detail could potentially be distracting. Having met thousands of people, I have seen countless home styles and family settings. I could easily become distracted by interior features, furnishings, or animals. But sights, sounds, and smells in a person's home or hospital room must never cause me to lose focus. Even strained family relationships must not divert my attention. Occasionally, a family member will apologize for some aspect of their dwelling, which highlights how my focus may be diverted from the patient. I remind them that I am not there to inspect their house. I have come to see their loved one. Everything else is inconsequential in that moment. This statement helps me stay focused, and helps focus the purpose of the visit.

How would our relationships—and for that matter, our lives—be different if we interacted with each person with this type of focus? Rather than judging a person by the stuff they have, we simply accept them as they are in that moment? When serving the person under hospice, it really does not matter what they possess. After all, they are leaving it all behind. So my interaction with them has nothing to do with their stuff, other than what it can tell me about who they are and what they value. My interaction has everything to do with them as a person. This makes all the difference.

When I speak with a patient, I let them set the agenda. I am careful not to steer off topic. I must be sensitive to subtle changes in their voice fluctuation, tone, or unfinished sentences. These nuances are often significant clues that there is either something worth further exploring or too painful to delve into deeper. Sometimes I don't know until I venture all so carefully into this area of deep personal experience. There are times

I have discovered a gold mine of rich, rewarding conversation because the person was at ease and comfortable in their reflections.

Relating with people is as much an art form as it is a science. No two people are exactly the same, and no person is exactly the same each time we meet. When is the last time you entered into a conversation without a set agenda? When is the last time you listened to understand instead of listened to respond? Too often, we converse with others with the hope of winning the argument rather than forming a connection.

Focus on Relationships

This kind of focus is important in personal relationships. Relating to others, even casually, requires focus. Like the athlete who loses focus during the competition, resulting in points for the other team, or the student who becomes distracted while taking a test, causing a lower score, so too in relationships. Unless we stay focused on relational priorities, the human connection suffers.

Have you ever been called out for not paying attention? The other person is telling you that your lack of focus signifies to them that you have more important priorities.

In the book, *The 5 Love Languages: The Secret to Love That Lasts*, author Gary Chapman details the importance of understanding another person's love language, that is, what motivates them. This understanding is paramount to the health of the relationship. Staying focused on the other person's love language is critical.

Human relationship is not a battle to be won or a challenge to be overcome. Rather, human relationship is intended to bring us pleasure. Let me say this again: human relationship is intended to bring us pleasure. So why do relationships cause us so much pain? Perhaps because we do not stay focused on their intended purpose.

Marriage was never intended to bring us frustration and pain, yet a large percentage of marriages experience both. Marriage should bring us our greatest joy. However, it often causes us our deepest sorrow. Why? There are a number of reasons, but one main reason is a lack of focus.

What begins as a courtship, in which we long to spend every waking and sleeping hour together, can, over time, deteriorate to the point where we can hardly stand being in the same space. How do we get to this place? Perhaps one or both individuals have lost focus. Demands from working, raising children, and paying bills become top priority. These are all important, but in the marriage relationship, our spouse is to remain our most intimate and important human relationship.

The good news is that we don't have to stay here. We can refocus on the marriage relationship and begin to reestablish a loving bond. But it will require making a choice to be more focused on the relationship.

The relationship we have with our children, regardless of their age, is also intended to bring pleasure. But what happens along life's path? Change happens. Our children change and so do we. The changes in our children are obvious. We sort through pictures and we can easily identify their physical changes. However, we occasionally fail to recognize the changes that we have experienced.

As parents, we experience a number of changes, including the declining health and death of our parents, relocation within our careers, and increased responsibility. Each of these changes can take our focus away from marriage and family life.

With our own increased stress, we can place greater pressure on our son or daughter to mature more quickly than they are prepared to. Do we expect our young adult to know exactly what type of career they want by high school graduation? How old were you when you settled upon a career choice? Some of us are still trying to figure out what we want to be when we grow up.

Life is a journey and there is no direct path to the destination. Everyone, and that includes *every one*, has to navigate at least one detour, dead end, or roadblock along the way. Maintaining focus helps keep us on the road to our preferred future.

As parents, it is important for us to stay focused on the big picture of our children's entire life. I try not to measure our children's life by one segment of their journey. This includes their adolescent and young adult years. After all, would we want our entire lives to be judged by our formative years? Probably not. Staying focused on the big picture helps maintain our parental relationship.

Focus on Labor

What is the purpose in living? What makes for a meaningful life? Certainly, relationships are a major part of the equation to these questions. When we simply look at the biology of human life, we see that it points to relationships. But beyond human relationships, what activities help frame our purpose for living and a meaningful life?

The answer to that question depends upon whom you ask. What I find gives me purpose in life may not be true for you. I do believe that we all need to find purpose in our work—and I am not necessarily speaking of our jobs. Rather, I am referring to our life's work, what we are intrinsically motivated to do.

In the Biblical story of Creation we read, "The LORD God took the man and put him in the Garden of Eden to work it and take care of it" (Genesis 2:15). Work was not intended to be a punishment. Rather, it was intended to be a meaningful use of time in order to provide a pleasurable task. Work is not a curse; rather, it is one element that helps provide meaning to a person's life.

There are countless activities that give purpose to our life. Let us consider how meaningful work gives purpose. Sometimes it is our jobs that enable us to engage in meaningful tasks outside the workplace.

It is important to stay focused while at work. Imagine what the morning commute would be like if the person who painted the lane markers on the roadway lost focus, even for a minute. Chaos would ensue. What if the person who programmed the elevator did not pay attention to the schematic drawing, or the person mixing paint at the home improvement store failed to follow the prescribed mixture?

Stay

So what is your work, and how does staying focused make a difference? Whether you are an athlete, student, plumber, or heart surgeon, focus is essential. It is essential to you and to those being served.

In my work, the people I visit force me to stay focused. They are a constant reminder that what is most important is what is important right now. They do not have the luxury of looking at life through the lens of years to come. They are forced to look at what is most important right now. Often, during my visit, I will ask them what their greatest concern is today. Their response to this question has, on occasion, surprised me.

There was the gentleman who, two days before his death, stated that his greatest concern, at that moment, was teaching his wife how to do electronic banking. Think about that: the man is hours from death and his most pressing concern is his wife's ability to pay bills online. Then there was the elderly wife whose greatest concern was for her aging husband. Who would make him his meals after she died? She had provided this for him over the previous sixty years.

Recently, I visited a man who stated that his greatest concern, at that moment, was making it to his grandchild's sporting event later that day. Another man told me that his greatest concern was getting a haircut so he would look presentable in the casket. Can you imagine that: electronic banking, meal planning, youth sports, and a haircut were mentioned as the greatest concerns of the dying? What I thought might be their greatest concerns were not most pressing at all to them.

By staying focused, I have discovered what is most important to others. Rather than assuming I know what their greatest concern is, I simply ask and listen.

There are numerous clues or signs one can discover about the other person simply by staying focused. In business, this is part of calling references, asking questions, and gathering information. In politics, it is part of the vetting process. In recruiting and drafting, it is doing homework on a potential player. In a dating relationship, staying focused helps nurture a potential bond. It shows the other person that you care.

During a job interview, it is imperative that both the interviewer and job candidate stay focused on the purpose of the interview. Staying focused on the purpose of the interview leads to a more productive meeting. Small talk is great when you are discussing small matters. However, any subject of importance requires sustained focus.

Preparing for an interview is an important step in the hiring process. Before sending a resume, do research on the company. How long has it been in business? Is it a global or local company? What is its reputation in the market place? How financially stable is the company and what is an acceptable pay range? Has this company been laying off or adding employees? These are just a few questions to ask prior to the interview.

The company also has a responsibility to thoroughly vet the potential candidate. Check with local, state, and federal laws regarding permissible background checks. Hiring the wrong person for the job requires too many valuable resources. A bad hire drains energy and thwarts momentum from both the company and your staff.

After nineteen years at the same agency, I have observed staff be hired that exhibited behaviors that they were not a good fit. Yet, the agency continued to extend them patience even though their skill set or personality traits did not align with the work.

If, after sufficient training, a new hire is not working out, it is in the best interest of all parties that an exit agreement be provided. The sooner the better. Remember, the business must stay focused on its mission, vision, and values. Staying focused during the interview process is an important first step in hiring the right personnel.

Too much time, energy, and financial resources are squandered attempting to get unfit, unqualified, or unmotivated staff up to an acceptable professional standard. Keys to workplace success include assembling the best team possible, allowing them to bring their best skill set to the task, providing autonomy, and expecting outstanding results.

In the book, *Built to Last*, author Jim Collins writes, "Those who build great companies understand that the ultimate throttle on growth for any great company is not markets, or technology, or completions, or products. It is one thing above all others: the ability to get and keep enough of the right people." Getting the right people will help the business stay focused in the long term.

Focus on Being Your Best Self

In 1987, I graduated from college and accepted my first job. I was hired as an assistant pastor at a church in northern Ohio. The starting salary was a $160.00 per week and the living accommodations consisted of a small apartment in the church-owned house.

When I arrived in town the first Friday of June, the apartment was empty. I did not have a piece of furniture to speak of. The pastor's wife placed a few phone calls to the members of the congregation and before the weekend was over, I had an old kitchen table, two metal folding chairs, a used orange plaid couch, a desk, and a twin bed. Welcome to ministry. This was the beginning of my career.

After Kim and I were married, we began to construct a life together as husband and wife. The dollars were few, but the love was plentiful. We had each other.

A year into our marriage, we thought it best to receive some counsel regarding our finances, as limited as they were. After a careful search, we invited a local certified financial planner to sit with us and offer her perspective. After a few minutes of introduction, including our income, she looked at us and said, "Is this all the money you have to work with?"

During the course of our conversation, the financial planner made a statement that I have never forgotten. As she spoke of the different types of financial investments available, she stopped mid-sentence and said, "The best investment you can make is an investment in yourselves." From that day forward, Kim and I have based many of our decisions on investing in ourselves. This investment has included additional formal education, healthy lifestyle choices, and trusted friendships. All have paid handsome dividends through the years.

I see firsthand the impact of not making this personal investment. I have met countless individuals who have succumbed to the negative effects of lifestyle choices. A month does not go by where I do not have a conversation with a person who says to me, "I want to live long enough to attend my daughter's wedding, to see my grandchild be born, or celebrate my anniversary."

I have never taken hope away from a person, regardless of how close death appears. However, there have been conversations that help the person take a realistic look at their current physical condition and the probability of them attending that all important event or family gathering. My goal is to help them live today so they can express their love while they still have the strength. Most people appreciate the conversation.

Anyone who has ever attempted to advance in their career, live a healthy life, and or maintain healthy relationships will tell you that it comes at a personal price. It takes focus and discipline to complete a course of study. It requires determination to make good food choices and stay active, especially as we age. Long-lasting, healthy relationships require commitment, intentionality, boundaries, and lots of forgiveness. Simply put, relationships require focus.

The dying person will draw strength from somewhere. It may be the love of another person, it may be their faith, or it may be their own inner determination. Often, it is a combination of several sources. But those who seem to do best are those who have a source of inner strength and focus. Remember, we finish life the way we have lived it.

What is it that you want to focus on in your own life? Do you want to get bigger, stronger, and faster? It will not happen through mental telepathy. Do you want to excel in a particular field? Then consider the "10,000 Hour Rule," which Malcolm Gladwell discusses in his book, *Outlier*. Gladwell writes that anyone who has achieved success in their particular field has done so because of their willingness to put in the time necessary to excel. According to Gladwell, achievement is talent plus preparation. He proposes that it takes 10,000 hours of practice in order to excel in any particular field.

Do you want to be a great spouse, parent, or partner? It will take time and effort. You cannot relate to your loved one by proxy and expect to have a strong bond. Do you want to be the top performer in your field? It will require sacrifice and dedication. Only the climbers who are willing to put in the practice make it to the summit. There is no replacement for time spent in the gym, at the studio, or with your craft. It takes time, dedication, and intent. Simply put, it takes focus.

Decide what you want to excel at and begin to work toward that goal. You cannot excel at everything, but you can become proficient in a particular skill, if you are willing to focus. As Steve Jobs said, "People think focus means saying yes to the thing you've got to focus on. But that's not what it means at all. It means saying no to the hundred other goods ideas that there are. You have to pick carefully. I'm actually as proud of the things we haven't done as the things I have done. Innovation is saying no to 1,000 things."

Focus on the Moment

During the 1992 US presidential debate between then Republican president George H. W. Bush; the Democratic challenger, Governor Bill Clinton; and businessman Ross Perot, much was made about President Bush's glancing at his watch during the debate. Pundits and critics depicted him as a tired—or worse yet, disinterested—candidate. Alex Markels, staff writer for *U.S. News & World Report*, wrote years later, "It was the telltale sign of a man made uneasy—or, at least, bored—by an audience member's question about how a deep recession had personally affected him. The then president's display of impatience seemed to speak volumes more than his awkward response."

What difference this glance at his watch made in the public's perspective of President Bush is debatable. However, the negative perception was broadcast in the media, and it set a narrative no candidate wants to defend. Bush was perceived by some to be uninterested in the hardships facing America, or at the very least, disingenuous in his voiced concern.

I do not wear a wristwatch. It has nothing to do with how it might interfere in my work; I simply do not like how it feels on my wrist. However, not having a wristwatch helps me stay focused in the moment.

Time has little bearing on how long I remain with a person. Their tolerance, their interest, and their receptivity determines the length of my stay.

Whether in business, personal relationships, or visiting the dying, people notice when we are distracted. It sends a signal, intentional or not, that other things are more important. It lessens our value in their minds and can hurt the relationship.

Several years ago, I served as a member on a youth ethics committee. The district supervisor occasionally sat in on our meetings in order to provide counsel. On more than one occasion, the supervisor pulled out his nail clippers and trimmed his fingernails. He was a man who had difficulty staying in the moment. This was a planning meeting, but he made it his personal grooming session.

Staying in the moment requires me to place a premium on what is happening in that moment. It requires me to value others with whom I am sharing that space. Staying in the moment sets a premium on this moment.

Focus on Quality—not Quantity

How long is too long? This is a great question. In the book *Bedside Manner*, author Katie Maxwell writes, "Short visits, (hospital or nursing home or home), can be just as good as longer ones. Look for indications that they (the patients) are growing tired or feeling badly. If they become restless or disinterested, it may be time to leave."

On November 19, 1863, President Abraham Lincoln delivered the Gettysburg Address. In less than 275 words, Abraham Lincoln captured the essence of the American experience of self-governance. The speech, while brief, remains one of our nation's greatest oratory selections. Like the speech, a hospital visit, business meeting, or consultation does not need to be long in order to be productive.

Several years ago, my supervisor called me into her office in order to discuss a number of work-related subjects including caseload, visit frequency, and the average length of my visits. In essence, it was a meeting about productivity. As the meeting progressed, she mentioned that the average length of time of my visits was considerably shorter than those of the other chaplains in our agency. She asked for an explanation. The only answer I could think of at the time is that I spend less time talking about peripheral issues and more time focused on what the person needs. I am not certain that she was convinced by my answer, but it was the only one I had. And my practice has not changed. The visit is not about length of time or topics covered. It is all about what the person's needs at that moment in time. It is about the quality of time you spend with the person to meet their needs, not the amount of time you spend. When I visit a person, I remain cognizant of his or her tolerance level. There is no minimal standard as to my length of stay. They set the agenda.

There are a few mental calculations I make whenever I visit the dying. Is the person sleepy, nauseous, or agitated? Are they visiting with a lifelong friend, family member, or other medical personnel? Are they watching their favorite television program or sporting event? People nearing the end experience a decreasing range of personal pleasures. If my visit takes one of the few remaining pleasures from them, then I have not served them. If I arrive at an ill-timed moment, I acknowledge it and offer to return at a later time. Most people insist that I remain. Understanding that I have a limited role in the person's life is important to remember. It helps me to stay just long enough to be helpful.

Just as important as knowing how long to stay is knowing how often to visit. The fictional character Dennis the Menace had a difficult time understanding this concept. Dennis's often-unwelcome visits caused his neighbor, Mr. Wilson, great anxiety. The age-old lesson here is, "Don't wear out your welcome." It is better to leave too early than to leave too late. Before I arrive at a person's home, I have an exit strategy. If someone has to ask me to leave, then I have stayed too long. Toward the end of my visit, I will often say that I want to honor the person's privacy. It is at this time that I ask them if there anything else I can offer. This question lets them know that I am sensitive to their needs.

Staying just long enough can apply to work and business as well. An employment separation can be complicated and messy when neither the employer nor the employee has an exit strategy. If you lost your job tomorrow, what would your strategy be? You might be surprised how your habits would change if you asked yourself this question at the end of each day. Regardless of how long you work for a company, everyone has a last day. Have an exit strategy. Stay just long enough.

Remember, you do not need to be with a company for many years in order for that time to be mutually beneficial. I often remind our new hires that we need them to decide from day one that they will make our agency better. It is important to know what you are doing and know how long you need to do it. One of the most difficult things to watch is someone being let go from a job or responsibility simply because they have stayed too long.

So how long is too long to stay at your current place of employment? This is the great question and one that only you can answer. There are indeed times when either the employee or the company need to move in different directions, but at the same time, sometimes we become anxious about workplace policies and look for an exit strategy. With a little patience you discover that, if you stay long enough, some of these policies change.

During my nineteen years in hospice care, I have worked with three different CEOs, numerous vice-presidents and directors of clinical services, along with various supervisors, managers, and coordinators. Sometimes the titles change as quickly as the newly hired person. As such, I have learned that it is important to learn how to take workplace directives in stride. Give it enough time and some of the new policies will be amended or outright abandoned. Workplace priorities today soon become distant memories, as Dumpsters across the country are filled with three-ring binders of the now-abandoned latest company initiative.

At the same time, it is important to realize that the business that fails to understand changing consumer demand may find its doors shuttered. Businesses that remain loyal to a particular product long after the customer has lost interest will burn through valuable capital. Sometimes a business can stay too long in a particular field and by so doing, compromise their market position. In the 1800s, there were over one hundred thousand blacksmiths in the United States. The demand was great and work was plentiful. When is the last time you used the services of a blacksmith?

Staying just long enough applies to relationships, too. How long do you stay in a relationship? Well, it depends on the relationship. A marriage takes a greater level of commitment than joining a bowling team. Unless, of course, you are a great bowler and a lousy lover!

Relationships are dynamic, ever changing. How much you invest in any relationship is personal. As a parent, I have invested my life in my children. As a chaplain, I have invested a great deal in my career; however, my work commitment pales in comparison to the one I have made to my wife and children.

There are several discoveries I have made while working with the dying. One is realizing who will be with us in our final hours. It will not be our boss, our mayor, or even our president. It will most likely be a loving spouse, child, or grandchild. These are the most lasting relationships.

How long do I stay with my wife? Till death do us part. How long do I stay on the bowling team? Until my sciatic nerve or rotator cuff acts up. How long do I stay at my job? Until one of us initiates a separation. It's that simple.

Staying focused helps give clarity to the question I posed earlier, "What is your greatest concern today?" When we see time for what it is, we have a better chance of staying focused in the moment. Time is a limited resource, and once we have used it up, it cannot be replenished.

Focus on Others

The first time I was the sole team member present at a patient's death came within the first few months on the job. I was asked to visit a fifty-four-year-old woman named Mandy. Our other team members had already visited earlier in the day, so I knew there were no other staff members scheduled.

As I entered the home, two things were apparent. First, Mandy was actively dying. Second, I knew that I was there for the duration.

15

Regardless that I was a hospice neophyte, there was no leaving this family.

Within ten minutes of arriving in the home, and following a brief prayer, Mandy breathed her final breath. As I stood bedside with her husband, Roger; their adult daughter, Katie; and two close friends, Sal and Marie, it was humbling to know that I, a complete stranger, was allowed to be present at the moment of Mandy's death. Here was one of the most sacred moments in the life of this family and I had the privilege to share in it.

Roger, Katie, Sal, and Marie began comforting one another. During this time, I noticed that the oxygen concentrator, which provides comfort by maintaining oxygen levels, was still running. Concentrators have a certain rhythm to their sound that can be mesmerizing and, at times, a bit annoying. Mandy had just died, so the concentrator was no longer providing any benefit. It would have been medically permissible for me to walk over and push the "off" button on the machine, but I refrained. Something instinctively kept me from doing that simple act.

Following the hugs and tear-filled moments, a few phone calls were placed in order to inform close family members of the death. I placed a call to our office informing them of the death, at which time they dispatched one of our nurses, who would come to pronounce the death and prepare the body for transfer. Again, I noticed that the concentrator was still running, yet I still did not feel it was my place to turn it off.

I am certain that it was less than ten minutes, though it seemed longer, that the concentrator continued operating to no personal benefit. Again, I considered walking over and turning off the unit, but I wanted to be sensitive to what Roger needed in that moment. Within a few minutes, he looked over at the concentrator and said out loud for all of us to hear, "As a last act of service for Mandy, I am going to turn off this machine."

In that moment, my earlier hesitancy to turn off the concentrator finally made sense. I could easily have rationalized why I should have turned off the concentrator. But I didn't. And that made all the difference. Being sensitive to others provides an environment where something special can occur. It means paying attention to others so that you know both what to do and what *not* to do.

There is no one script on how to focus on others. Focusing on others requires a willingness to listen, speak, think, act, move, be still, arrive, depart, stand up, sit down, touch, refrain from touching, and the list goes on and on. But over the course of my career, I have learned a few things that have helped me better focus on others.

Focus on Collaboration

In both our personal and professional lives there are opportunities to do things that are well within our capabilities; however, let me suggest that you consider not only your abilities, but also the abilities of those within your circle of influence. Not every job is yours to fulfill, not every assignment is yours to accept. Perhaps there is someone within your family or work environment who needs the opportunity, like Roger above, to participate in the process. After all, that is what made the difference for both Roger and me.

Many businesses emphasize to their employees the importance of workplace collaboration. At my workplace, we truly practice the team concept. Each person under hospice care is assigned a medical doctor, registered nurse (RN), certified nurse assistant (CNA), social worker, and chaplain. The person is required by law to receive a doctor's order for service. They are also required to have regular visits from a nurse. They have the option of accepting the CNA, social worker, and chaplain, though most people under hospice accept all the disciplines.

Do you carry an exorbitant amount of responsibility? What part of your current responsibilities can involve the help of others? Too much to do at home? How about enlisting your children or spouse in order to help with the household responsibilities? Not only does their involvement ease your burden, but it also teaches them important life skills. Too much to do at work? Are you the person who fixes the copier, makes the coffee, and develops company projections and policies? Good luck keeping that all going. You are working at an unsustainable pace. Something will eventually give; let's hope it's not you.

Do not misunderstand me, the work must get done. However, there is more than one path to the same destination. Our work can be meaningful, honorable, and accomplished with a collaborative spirit. But, it can be so much more rewarding when done in a manner that is sensitive to the needs of all people, including yourself.

Focus on Perspective

There is a well-travelled story about a passerby who happened upon three brick masons building a church. When the man asked the first worker what he was doing, the worker replied, "I'm laying brick." The man proceeded farther down the job site and asked another mason the same question. This man replied, "I am building a wall." Finally the man came upon a third mason and asked the same question. This man replied, "I am building one of the world's most beautiful cathedrals in which generations will come and experience the majesty of God." Three men doing the same work on the same structure, but each saw his work in a different light.

When I started working at hospice, I experienced a tremendous learning curve. I was trying to understand how to best serve the needs of the person while dealing with the mental and emotional stress. It became apparent during my first month that families really depend upon hospice for guidance and support. After all, dying is one of the few things in life that we don't get to practice. We just do it. However, we tend to do it better when we have an adequate support system. This is where hospice excels.

I wonder how we would approach our jobs if we saw ourselves in a similar light? People need what you have to offer. Someone might say, Come on, I push a broom for a living—or, I flip burgers—what value is there in doing that? Actually, there is great value in any task, when it is done well and with a broad perspective.

What is your work? Teaching children or influencing future generations? Trading commodities or feeding the world? Renting trucks or moving a nation and making dreams come true? It all depends upon one's perspective.

According to Henry Cloud, I once read, "People will think more highly of you for thinking more highly of them, and they will go to great lengths to regain your favorable opinion, if ever they loss it." Being sensitive to how others think and feel is not necessary in order to get along in life, but it is necessary in order to get along with others. Being sensitive to others does not require an extraordinary effort. It simply takes a willingness to make the effort—and the payoff is worth it. Being sensitive—that is, aware—can save time, money, a marriage, even another life. Someone who stays sensitive is someone who stays focused in the moment.

Focus on the Big Picture

One key to focusing on others is understanding the big picture. On a recent home visit, I met Tom, a retired fireman, who told me that what helped him succeed in his forty-year career is that whenever he went out on a call, he reminded himself that he did not cause the accident. He could be sensitive to the need without taking responsibility for having caused the problem.

I have learned that being sensitive to the needs of others does not mean that I fix every difficulty. Working with the dying, I have no fix. By being sensitive, I can help foster an environment where healing, forgiveness, love, and affirmation can be expressed. I can work with the dying person each day because it doesn't all fall to me. Rather, I am a part of a team.

At the same time, being sensitive is different from being emotional. In my work, I could cry every day. The heartache and grief that the people I visit carry could be overwhelming. While I am sensitive to the hurt, I am not necessarily emotionally invested. If I was emotionally attached to each person I visit, my career would have ended years ago due to the personal toll. One of the keys to longevity in any career is knowing how much of yourself to invest in your career. Think of your career more as a marathon and less as a sprint.

In professions such as sports, where the turnover is quick compared to other professions, it is wise to prevent injuries. A football player who goes all out all the time, even in practice, is not thinking about the long-term negative consequences. The average professional football career lasts approximately four years. The accumulative effect of head and body trauma is causing sports at all levels to rethink their priorities.

Have you ever known someone, who, after many years in a particular career, became jaded toward others? Who became emotionally insensitive from dealing with a particular problem? Like hands calloused from repetitive work, so too can we become hardened toward the people we serve. For instance, law enforcement agents deal with the moral ills in our society on a daily basis. Their work requires them to serve in some unimaginable situations. It is little wonder that anyone chooses this as their career. However, hundreds of thousands of people do this job every day. I imagine that only those who are a part of this fraternity, who share that bond of service, fully understand the burden that comes when you take the oath and put on the badge. But I also imagine they get through it because they focus on the big picture.

Focus on the Silence

When attending a death, I remain pretty quiet. That is saying a lot, seeing how, for me, conversation comes easy. In his book, *Leading With The Heart: Coach K's Successful Strategies for Basketball, Business, and Life*, Mike Krzyzewski, Duke University head basketball coach, described visiting his dear friend, Jim Valvano, the day he died (April 28, 1993). Krzyzewski captured the sense of what it is like to be in the presence of someone who is dying.

Coach K wrote, "A coach is supposed to know what to do. But I had no clue what to do. I felt like I was no help to anybody. I believe my being there was comforting to Pam [Jim's wife], but I felt like I should have faded into the wall. I felt so powerless to do anything that might have been of consequence during those next few moments."

While Coach K has much more experience courtside than at the bedside of a dying person, he captured the essence of what I experience every time I attend a death. Words are hard to come by and should be used judiciously. I only engage in appropriate conversation when the family is receptive. Otherwise, I keep quiet.

Focus on Others' Stories

I enjoy hearing people tell their life stories. I find the human story most compelling, better than fictional writing or a television broadcast. What I have observed when hearing someone's life story is how their challenges and opportunities have brought them to their current life setting.

So many in the health care profession tell of how early in their life, either they or a family member were ill and required medical care. The desire to help others was conceived in their hearts and a career of helping others was pursued. Those who enlist in the military have often been influenced by an event or person whom they admire. They have become sensitive to country, honor, and duty. First responders, many who early in life saw the value of helping others, courageously and sacrificially serve their community.

People who are sensitive to the needs of others can be found in every occupation including cooks, custodians, accountants, teachers, the sciences, and the arts. I would submit that this sensitivity has, in large part, led them into their current field. Sensitivity, courage, tenacity are not qualities listed on a resume, but their value is without measure. Competence, training, and skill are essential; however, they do not give the whole picture. Show me a person who is sensitive to the needs of others, courageous, tenacious, and competent, and I will show you someone who will succeed in life.

How do we measure the intangibles? They are woven into the fabric of our life story. In my experience, knowing someone's life story is a better indicator of their potential for success than items listed on their resume. Consider any notable person in world history and you will most likely find an incredible, compelling life story. Each one has a story prior to their rise to prominence. Consider your life story and how it has shaped the person you have become. Allow your story to influence and help those you meet along the way.

Focus on the Subtle

When talking with a dying person, it is often the subtle references in a conversation that, if further explored, have proven to be the most fruitful.

Betty was a ninety-four-year-old, bed-bound nursing-home patient. At my first and only visit, she told me about her late husband, her siblings, and other family members. She mentioned that today was her only surviving brother's birthday. She knew, due to his failing health, that she would not see him on his birthday. I detected slight disappointment in her voice, but there was nothing I could do to get him to the nursing home. I also knew that this would be the last birthday she would have with her brother due to her pending death. Prior to leaving her room, I offered a prayer for her and her brother.

As I walked down the hallway, I thought about my cell phone. I reentered Betty's room and told her that we were calling her brother in order to wish him a happy birthday. I could see in her eyes a look of excitement and confusion. You see, she had never used a cell phone.

I dialed her brother's home number and handed her the phone. Not knowing what to do with the phone, she held it like it was a walkie-talkie. I showed her how to hold the phone, and she offered her brother a birthday greeting. They talked for about thirty seconds before she said in her frail voice, "Well, I better go, this is costing a lot of money." I waved my hands and told her to take her time and enjoy the conversation. After another thirty seconds, she bid him farewell and handed me the phone.

Before I left her room for the second time, Betty thanked me for the kind offer. We laughed about the shared moment and I went on my way. Three days later, Betty died.

Like Betty, Sally was also in our hospice, living in another local nursing home. She was born and raised in the community and would share with me some of her favorite memories. Sally was seventy-two years old and slowly declining. On one of my visits, she began to speak of a local restaurant that is known for its poor-boy sandwiches. Her mouth was almost salivating as she talked about how delicious they tasted.

Prior to leaving the facility, I checked with her nurse in order to see if she could have a poor-boy sandwich. The next day, just prior to the lunch hour, I entered her room with a poor-boy sandwich, extra garlic. Her eyes were like saucers. She cleared her bedside table and I placed the sandwich before her. Sally invited me to have some of the sandwich, but I declined and told her that I was going to leave so she could enjoy it.

In my subsequent visits, Sally would talk about how good that sandwich tasted. It was a comfort knowing that something so simple could mean so much. Within the next two months, Sally would continue her physical decline and eventually pass. But not before eating her favorite sandwich one last time.

Henry was a seventy-eight-year-old man who also lived in a nursing home. Due to the effects of cancer, he was experiencing decreased strength. His placement in the nursing home was due to his wife's inability to provide the necessary care. Henry was personable and kind, and he had a curious mind. He really enjoyed playing card games, especially Cribbage. On one of my visits, he attempted to teach me how to play. Unfortunately, I did not pick up the rules.

During one of my visits, he mentioned that he wasn't too fond of the nursing home food. He made a remark about the simple pleasure of a good hamburger. He wasn't asking for one; rather, he was simply making conversation.

As I concluded my visit, I checked with his nurse in order to confirm that he could eat a burger, and then I proceeded to the local burger joint. Within the hour, I was back in Henry's room with a hot and tasty steak burger. Like Sally, I left him alone so he could enjoy his food. As with Betty and Sally, Henry also succumbed to the effects of the disease soon thereafter.

Three individuals finishing their life's journey. None of them asked me for anything. Yet, each one accepted a simple gesture of kindness. Did it change their prognosis? No, but for a moment, it changed their perspective. In that moment, they could find pleasure in a final birthday greeting or a hot sandwich.

Did it require much effort to retrieve the cell phone from my car? Was my schedule so tight that I could not deliver a poor-boy or steak burger?

Focusing on others does not take a herculean effort. It simply takes a willingness to listen and respond.

Some Final Thoughts on Staying Focused

So how can we be successful in human relationships? How can we find success in our work, our leisure, or for that matter, any endeavor? The answer is, stay focused. Staying focused is a common denominator in finding satisfaction in relationships, achievement in business, and success in life.

The husband and wife who truly make each other their top priority will navigate any challenge life may bring, and life brings challenges. They will focus on their relationship, but they will give each other their space. Maintaining healthy personal boundaries is beneficial in any relationship. Healthy relationships, like healthy plants, need room to grow. On the other hand, show me a husband and wife who have drifted away from making their marriage a top priority, and I will show you a marriage at risk.

The business that stays focused on its core competencies, given the business is relevant, will be successful. Understand that customers do need to eat at your restaurant every night in order for yours to be their favorite. The Goose Island Beer Company's slogan states, "We don't need to be the only beer you drink. We just want to be the best beer you drink." Here is a company that understands and values their customer. On the other hand, the business that abandons its integrity, initiative, and ingenuity is a business that will eventually lose its influence in the market.

Whether you experience a medical crisis, unemployment, or a broken relationship, the best thing to do is to stay focused. Regardless of how desperately we would like to move past the difficulty and onto the solution, there is no fast track pass the challenge.

Something is to be gained as we journey through the experience. It's the courage within and connection with others that becomes evident. Neither would be fully realized without the experience. When we wish away the days, even the difficult ones, we are wishing away our life.

Questions

1. Who is the most focused person that you know? How does this focus help them be successful?
2. In your opinion, is the ability to remain focused more of a learned trait or genetic?
3. Of the many personal accomplishments in world history, name one that you find most remarkable. Why do you find this particular accomplishment most remarkable?
4. Name a personal accomplishment that required you to remain focused. Did you discover this to provide a sense of personal satisfaction? Why or why not?
5. Do you find it more difficult beginning a particular project or finishing one? Why do you think this is so?

Chapter Two: Stay Calm

I admire first responders—police, firefighters, paramedics, crisis counselors, 911 operators—all those who perform at their best when the rest of society is facing its worst. I hold these people in highest regard because they know how to remain calm in emergency situations.

Airline pilots specifically are trained for emergency situations, when they must maintain altitude above all else during in-flight emergencies. Cockpit recordings have validated this important element. There have been occasions when flight crews have neglected the plane's flight pattern and altitude due to distractions caused by cockpit warning lights or alarms. This oversight has resulted in disaster for both aircraft and occupants.

But there are others who, though perhaps not officially recognized as such, deal with emergencies daily. Recently I met Barry, a retired tow-truck driver, who was receiving care under our hospice. I had never considered tow-truck drivers part of the first responder team; however, after hearing some of Barry's work experiences, I have come to better appreciate their irreplaceable role in crash scene recovery.

Daily I interact with and support the dying, but seldom does my work involve sudden trauma. By the time I meet someone, they have had time to consider their prognosis. Occasionally, there are times when the medical diagnosis has just been received and the person and family are attempting to process the implications. Nevertheless, I have learned that staying calm isn't only important during an emergency, but also within any given relationship, staying calm is important to the health of the relationship. Some people maintain a calmer disposition than others. What role environment, genetics, or simply making a choice has in our staying calm is debatable. Staying calm helps foster an atmosphere where the necessary support can be provided. Most of my visits involve families that are calm, though there are occasions when I encounter crisis in the home. I can offer little support if, during these crisis situations, I am unable to stay calm.

There are several key elements to staying calm.

Understand Your Role

We are responsible for our obligations, but before we can carry them out, we need to understand our roles. In my field, I am responsible for providing pastoral support to the person and his or her loved ones. For instance, I might lose my calm in a person's home if asked to insert a catheter, dispense medication, or provide wound care. Why? Because these are all outside my role.

One of the keys to remaining calm in any situation is to ask, "What is my role in this situation?" Just as there are professional boundaries in every position, there are personal boundaries in every relationship. Not every burden is yours to carry, not every problem is yours to solve. Let me rephrase this: you don't have to do it all. You're not Superman or Wonder Woman.

This idea can be especially difficult for those in a supervisory or parental role. One of a parent's most challenging questions is how much to do for their child at the various stages of the child's development. For example, it's okay to hold your child's hand as they are learning to walk or crossing an intersection. However, if you're still holding their hand when they are married with their own children, then, may I suggest, there is a personal boundary issue. Some parents never stop walking ahead of their children in an attempt to remove every obstacle. If given the choice, these parents would wrap their child in bubble wrap, lest an injury beset the child. But is this really your role as a parent?

I am a parent to our three adult children. However, I do not parent them to the same extent that I did when they were toddlers. My wife, Kim, and I have prepared them to the best of our ability. What they decide to do with our efforts is up to them. Will they experience setbacks, disappointments, and failures? Most certainly, but these challenges are not unique to them. They are common human experiences.

At the same time, I do not resent helping our children when they ask. I have spent my entire adult life helping others. Why would I refuse to help our own children? While I have helped them at various times as they transition into adulthood, I remind them that helping them when they are twenty-two years old is different than helping when they are forty-two years old. I will not be as gracious if, when they are forty-two, they call me asking for gas money. Our plan is that our role as parents will change with the passing of time. That is good for us, but best for them.

Understanding my role helps everyone keep calm. For example, as a supervisor at a workplace, it is important to understand your role. You are responsible for creating a safe environment, where mutual respect is demonstrated. You are responsible for ensuring that your staff has both the training and tools to be successful. Once you have secured these elements for your staff, it is up to them to perform. If they are not performing, then you are responsible for evaluating them. It may require more training, better equipment, or a safer environment. But remember, they are responsible for fulfilling their role just as you are responsible for fulfilling yours. If either of these are not occurring, then change is inevitable.

Once the workplace supervisor is clear on his or her role, the job becomes less stressful. It is the responsibility of the supervisor to clearly define workplace expectations and have the courage to follow through. Many supervisors make the work environment unduly stressful because they do not supervise. Rather, they act as a pirate, a parent, or a patron: too harsh, too kind, or too patronizing.

There is one particular situation I encounter in my profession often that requires me to know my role. My particular region of the country has a large Roman Catholic population. On occasion people will ask me if I am a Catholic priest. They usually ask this question within the context of the dying person receiving a visit from the priest. In the Catholic Church, only a Catholic priest can administer the sacrament of the anointing of the sick. I explain to the person that I am not a Catholic priest; however, I can contact one on their behalf. I know that my role as chaplain is not to act as a pseudo priest, rabbi, or imam, and understanding this allows me, and those being served, the ability to stay calm. I don't pretend to be someone I am not.

Another situation that happens to me often is that, when visiting residents who live in nursing homes, someone might ask me if I am a medical doctor. In fact, there are occasions when a nurse or doctor will say, "Hello, Doctor." I simply tell them I am not a doctor; I am a chaplain. Understanding my role and clearly communicating it to others helps keep the calm.

Clarify Expectations

One of the great challenges within any organization—or any relationship, for that matter—is clearly communicating expectations. We assume that the new supervisor will have the same expectations as her predecessor or that the staff are all aware of the company's expectations. However, unless expectations are clearly conveyed, people often draw their own conclusions. The military has a saying about this situation: "If you do not inform the troops, they will inform themselves." People cannot read minds, so clarify expectations.

In your house, which way does the toilet paper come off the roll? This is a question that often divides people. I am of the mind that the paper should roll over the top. But what does this have to do with staying calm? Nothing really, but it does illustrate the need to clarify expectations. Several years ago my friend, Patty, invited her mother, Marge, to move in with her husband and children. Patty mentioned to me that one irritating habit Marge had was how she placed the toilet paper roll on the holder. Marge would place it on the holder roll side along the wall. Patty and the other family members would take it off and "fix it" so that the paper rolled over the top. Even after several years of adjusting the toilet paper, Marge continued to place it on the holder the "wrong way."

Why did this continue to happen? Patty never clarified her expectations.

If you need something, speak up. If someone is not doing their job properly, then take the time to teach them. If someone is new to your company, assume that they do not know how you want something done. Even if it's as insignificant as toilet paper.

Within the health care field, hospice care providers seem to attract a certain type of person. However, even among hospices, employee expectations differ. Our particular hospice has seen a great influx of nurses in recent years, whereas in my first fifteen years there was very little nurse turnover. Now the need for new hire orientation is more pronounced.

Regardless of the rate of turnover in any particular field, it is important to clearly convey your company's expectations. One way to do that is writing expectations in a policy manual; however, this cannot be the only step. These policies should be regularly highlighted and modeled by all staff, especially senior management.

Another important step in workplace efficiency is helping your staff to work within their defined roles and responsibilities. I am not suggesting that employees cannot be cross-trained for greater effectiveness or to understand other roles. I am suggesting that, as I mentioned above, chaplains should not be starting IVs. Companies that help foster a greater degree of calm among their workforce are those who respect their employees' fields of expertise.

Clarifying expectations also sometimes means remaining silent when you could speak. Have you ever spoken on behalf of your spouse or a coworker without their knowledge? What happened? You probably received a reprimand. Why? Because you committed them to something without their knowledge. Sometimes we create our own problems by speaking for others without their permission, and in turn we forfeit the calm simply because we speak when we should remain quiet. Having an opinion and sharing an opinion are two distinct things.

There are other times when we place ourselves in the middle of something that is none of our business. You have heard the phrase, "Sticking your nose where it does not belong"? I wonder how much calm we forfeit because we act outside our role of responsibility.

Working with thousands of families during the past nineteen years, I have encountered all types of family function and dysfunction. Never once have I attempted to change or challenge particular family dynamics, because it is not my role to act as referee.

Marilyn was a 90-year-old woman who was being cared for by her daughter Janice. During my first and only visit, Marilyn and Janice shared with me the heartache Marilyn felt due to an estranged relationship with her other daughter, Teri. Teri made little effort to remain in contact with Marilyn, even though Marilyn attempted on many occasions to reconcile. At the same time, Janice, who had cared for Marilyn, was angry toward Teri because of the lack of involvement and respect shown their mother. As they shared their story, I simply listened and empathized.

The following week, Marilyn died, and Janice called Teri in order to give her the option to see their mother one last time before she was removed from the house and taken to the crematorium. Teri accepted Janice's offer. A request was placed for a chaplain to be present when both sisters were together. Due to my being out of the office on that particular day, our agency sent another chaplain, Brett. Brett knew nothing of the long-standing family dynamics.

Upon my return to work the following day, Brett informed me, with deep regret, that he had tried to negotiate a reconciliation between Janice and Teri. His approach was to suggest that Janice, who had cared for their mother, extend forgiveness toward her estranged sister, Teri. Needless to say, his effort was not well received.

Brett failed to understand that these siblings had a long-standing feud that was, at the moment, irreconcilable. It did not matter that their mother's dead body lay in the next room. Death does not foster reconciliation. In fact, it often exacerbates the schism.

Do you want to keep the calm? Then sometimes you need to keep quiet. Not every problem is yours to fix. We can only lead people where they want to go. Understanding your role and clarifying expectations helps keep the calm.

Ask for—and Accept—Help

Another key to maintaining the calm is knowing when to ask for help. I cannot tell you how many anxious days I have spent attempting to take care of something outside the arena of my personal skill set. You name it, I have tried to fix it. From broken cars, to electronics, to relationship issues. Some of the problems I could address. However, many required the help of someone with the proper training and tools. The sooner I came to accept my limitations, the better off for everyone involved, myself included.

Daily I face problems that are bigger than I am. Every person I visit has a problem: they are dying. I cannot solve their problem, nor can I change their reality. And in fact, no one has ever asked me to fix their problem. It's true. No one has ever asked me to make them well. I have never been asked to do what is beyond my ability. People are just grateful that I acknowledge their problem, affirm them as a person, and remain available. The sooner they accept it, the sooner the possibility for calm. I have yet to meet a person who denies their medical prognosis and is calm; rather, those who refuse to accept their terminal diagnosis remain in a state of distress and anxiety. I know personally that facing my problems does not cause me to lose my calm. In fact, acknowledging that the problem is bigger than I am actually brings a calm because it keeps me from thinking that I am responsible for fixing the problem.

Most people—regardless of their gender, race, or social status—want to take care of themselves. They want to maintain their autonomy. They want to have a voice in what happens to them. The people who best maintain their calm are those who simply accept the available help. Compare that person to the one who resists the available help. They decline the assistance of the medical staff, equipment, or medication, and by so doing, they create stress for themselves and their loved ones.

I often say to a family member, "If your loved one is restless, then everyone in the house is restless. If your loved one is calm, then so is the family." Refusing the available support makes life more difficult for the patient, their loved ones, as well as the health care professional.

Consider your current life setting. Are you feeling restless, agitated, or uneasy? What is the cause? Are there things occurring in your life that are beyond your control? Ask yourself what help you need that will solve the problem. You might be surprised how simple the answer is. For example, many of our hospice patients could do themselves a world of good if they simply took the prescribed medication. Instead, they resist taking the medicine or they believe that there is virtue in suffering. Either option can create problems. By resisting this available help, they cause themselves and their families' anxiety, and they place an unnecessary strain on the medical staff. All of this could be avoided with a little prevention. In hospice, we see firsthand how, "An ounce of prevention is worth a pound of cure."

So what's your biggest concern today? Have you at least acknowledged it? Have you done anything to prevent it or solve it? Are you willing to accept the offer of help? This is the place to begin. If the problem is beyond your ability to solve, then look around and see who might be able to help. Good help is closer than you think. It may be a neighbor, a classmate, a coworker, or a stranger that holds the answer. Too often, we overthink someone's offer to help. Do yourself a favor and simply accept the help.

The challenge for most of us is in the asking for help. We like being the solution for someone else; however, most of us are reluctant to ask for help for ourselves. The grace to receive is more closely linked to the grace to give than some of us are willing to accept. I see this grace as two sides of the same coin. I have discovered that, in asking for help, a bond can be developed or strengthened. For example, asking help from your spouse, child, or grandchild can have a positive effect on the relationship. It is the acknowledgment of your need and the help of others that acts as a bonding agent in further strengthening the love and respect.

I experienced this firsthand when my father was dying. He became more dependent upon others for the simplest tasks, but his need for assistance strengthened the bond of love and trust like nothing prior. He relied upon our help in driving him to his doctor's appointments, getting up out of a chair, and eventually administering pain medicine. While it was difficult for us to switch roles, this dependence helped foster a greater love and respect within our family. No experiences, especially the difficult ones, are ever wasted if we choose to learn from them. The lessons he taught me of interdependence and reliance upon others are ones that I still draw upon, and I am certain that I will draw upon them in my final days.

Recently I visited Chet, an older gentleman, who had served his local church in a variety of roles spanning over fifty years. He was actively involved in his community and found great satisfaction in helping others. Now, due to his declining health, all he could do was sit in his recliner most of the day. He acknowledged that he found little value in the dying process. He preferred his life to be over rather than slowly succumb to the disease. Similarly, a few weeks before my father died, he looked at me said, "I don't agree with the actions of Kevorkian"—referring to Dr. Jack Kevorkian—"however, I now have a better understanding of those who do." My father was finding it difficult to see any value in his suffering. However, I often remind the dying person of the invaluable lessons they are providing for their family—one of which is how to ask for and accept help. The parent has spent a lifetime teaching their children how to live life. Now they are teaching them how to finish life.

Accepting help from others outside of your immediate family and friends can be critical in solving your greatest need. But we have all received help from a complete stranger—from the nurse at the hospital who cleaned us seconds after birth, to the school bus driver, to the person at the Department of Motor Vehicles. Help from strangers occurs throughout our lives. We just don't recognize them as strangers.

Asking for a little help from above never hurts either. The person who has a faith in God, or a higher power, tends to face this final challenge with a greater calm. Not all religious people are the model of peace and tranquility, but of all the people that I have met, in general, those who have a faith base tend to cope better than those who have none.

For some, no amount of convincing will cause a change of mind about the reality of a God, a higher power, or whatever name people ascribe to a greater spiritual being. I am certain, after years of living with the dying, that there is something that orchestrates even the smallest details of our lives. I have watched firsthand as people, events, and circumstances come together at just the right moment without explanation or human influence. Some may call this coincidence, luck, or just pure chance. However, spend a week working with the dying, and I am convinced that you will see things differently. I look from a different vantage point. I see a God who is mindful of all people, but especially the dying person. While I cannot explain it, I know it is true.

Regardless of where the source of help comes from—family, friend, or faith tradition—accepting help goes a long way in alleviating stress. The next time you find yourself in a difficult situation, stop and consider where the source of help may come from. You might be surprised.

See the Big Picture

Sometimes we fail to stay calm because of our myopic view of a situation. We become so obsessed with a particular detail of the project or person that we see little else. Don't misunderstand me: we need detail-oriented people in the world. Most of the great accomplishments in world history have come about as a result of focused intention, from scientific research to space exploration, medical advancements to how humans interact. Most of our current understandings have come through deliberate and detailed focus. But in general, the micro view finds balance when considered with the macro view, and vice versa.

This dual view can often get lost. We can become so obsessed with our particular agenda that we lose sight of the big picture. We can lose our calm in negotiating a business deal or discussing our religious beliefs. We tend to look through one set of lenses. For instance, we can become incensed or irritated with someone solely based on their opinion of civic responsibility or their preference for a particular rock band. But when faced with our mortality—and I mean really faced with our mortality—so many of the concerns we carry in life fade away. I learned early on that the dying person spends little time, if any, arguing about the best basketball player or guitarist of all time, or even their particular religious beliefs.

Yet many of us find it difficult to see the big picture. If you spend all your attention on your company's stock price, then you may be tempted to violate your personal or professional integrity. If you are attempting to win a religious or political exchange at any cost, be careful, lest you win the argument and lose a friend.

One way to see the big picture is to back away from the situation. Have you ever flown over your neighborhood in an airplane? On a recent return flight home, we were descending into our local airport on a flight pattern that goes directly over our town. As I looked out of the airplane window, several realities became apparent, realities that are not apparent from ground level. The problem is, this is where we live life. Seeing my neighborhood from above helped me gain a better understanding of the topography, population density, and smallness of the houses. I saw my immediate living environment in a whole new light. This is the advantage gained by backing away from a situation.

How might your company—or for that matter, your career—benefit from seeing the big picture? How might your relationships improve if you occasionally took a step back and viewed them from a different perspective?

Several years ago, I visited Sharon, a thirty-six-year-old wife and mother of four children. Sharon was dying of cancer. During my first and only visit, Sharon looked at me and asked, "Why would God give me four children and not allow me to raise them?" Sharon's life was coming to end and she had questions. I had few answers. I simply said, "I do not know why, but I believe that they will always have your love and values. That they will never forget you and your life will go on in each of them."

The very next week I visited Dan, a thirty-eight-year-old husband and father of four children. Like Sharon, he was also dying from cancer. As if rehearsed, Dan looked at me and said, "Why would God give me four children and not allow me to raise them?" Two different individuals within one week asked me the exact same question.

Was my answer any better for Dan than it was for Sharon? No. I simply said, "I do not know why, but I believe that they will always have your love and values. They will never forget you and your life will go on in each of them."

The only answer I knew to offer both Sharon and Dan was one in which we had to look at the big picture of their children's future. After all, their life was coming to a fast-approaching conclusion.

Within the month both Sharon and Dan died. How their spouses and children navigated such loss is still a mystery to me. But I know that their children still have their parents' love and values, and I believe that they think of their deceased parents every day.

Parents face many challenges with their children. However, when we consider the big picture of life, love, and loss, many of these challenges become more manageable, or at least more bearable.

A few months after my father's retirement, and just prior to his diagnosis, my older brother was laid off from his job. My father was sixty-seven years old and had a retirement pension. My brother was forty years old with two small children. One afternoon our family had gathered for a birthday party and I asked my brother if he would rather be sixty-seven, retired with a pension, or forty and out of work. He looked at me, laughed, and said, "Forty and out of work." My brother understood that, even though he had been laid off, the big picture of his life was still positive.

When is the last time, when faced with a real difficulty, you took a step back and looked at the problem from another perspective? Being able to see how your current challenge looks in light of life's bigger picture often brings a calm.

Rest from Your Work

When is the last time you took a vacation from your vocation? When is the last time you disconnected mentally, emotionally, and physically from your work? One of the keys to staying calm when we are at work is disconnecting from those demands when we are away from work.

I realize that some people have jobs, or bosses, that are incredibly demanding. Others, because of your specialized training or position of ownership, need to be available 24/7. But this does not mean that you need to be on high alert. It's not practical, but more importantly, it's not healthy.

There are people whose minds never turns off work. They are in a constant state of mental and emotional engagement. Even on their vacation, they are answering emails and texts, and planning the next big idea. For those who own a business, the ability to get away from thinking about work is especially difficult.

In the bestselling book *Seven Habits of Highly Effective People*, the late Stephen Covey writes, "Habit 7 is personal PC. It's preserving and enhancing the greatest asset you have—you. It's renewing the four dimensions of your nature—physical, spiritual, mental, and social/emotional...'Sharpen the saw' basically means expressing all four motivations. It means exercising all four dimensions of our nature, regularly and consistently in wise and balanced ways." Covey quantifies the value in taking the time to stop and sharpen the blade rather than continuing with a dull blade.

When is the last time you stopped long enough to rest, reflect, and "sharpen the saw"? Several years ago, a local rabbi named Daniel presented a workshop at our agency. During his presentation, Daniel made a comment that I have not forgotten. Referring to Shabbat, or the Sabbath, Daniel said that we have fifty-two holidays scheduled into every calendar year, yet we often complain of being exhausted from the pace and demands of life. His point being, it's not that we do not have opportunity to rest; we simply fail to recognize and take advantage of it.

Our ability to stay calm at the workplace is often dependent upon our ability to refresh, recharge, and renew. Sometimes we feel stressed at work because we did not take the time to rest when we were away from work. Our days off are filled with household chores, trips to care for ailing family members, and our children's competitions. If you spend four hours on Sunday evening driving home from your daughter's weekend tournament, chances are you will feel a bit stressed come Monday morning. It's difficult to bring our best self to work when we gave it away the night before.

We need to find a work/life balance that allows us to be our best self, especially when we are at work. After all, last time I checked, it was work, not leisure, that enables us to make the mortgage payment, buy the groceries, and pay for our child's education.

Disconnecting from the demands of life can be a challenge. However, there are a number of ways to renew the body, mind, and spirit. Options are as varied as a weekend retreat to a ten-minute hot shower. What is important is taking the time to clear your mind, calm your spirit, and relax your body. Experiencing renewal does not need to be expensive or extensive. It does need to be intentional and experiential.

Have a Plan

I have come to understand that the people who tend to stay calm are those who have a plan. They have made their final wishes known, including but not limited to the following: What is to happen to their body once they have died? Will they be cremated or have a full burial? Who will care for the body—a funeral home, cremation or anatomical society? Will there be a wake, memorial service, or private committal? How will these services be paid for?

Those who have talked to their family about any assets or liabilities tend to have a more peaceful death. Years ago there was a syndicated radio show called "Money Matters" with the late Larry Burkett. He often said something to the effect of, "Do your giving while you're living so you're knowing where it is going."

What is true in living is true in dying. A cluttered mind leads to a cluttered life. Many families do not talk about assets and liabilities until after their loved one is dead. My experience has taught me that those who stay calm are those who have a plan and share it.

Consider the opposite to a well-ordered life. That is, the person who seldom has a plan for most anything. They waltz through life rarely giving serious thought to the next day, let alone the next year. Their organizational efforts are minimal, and they have trouble finding a matching pair of socks. They fly by the seat of the pants and see life as this great adventure. They are what we call an "esprit libre," or a "free spirit."

While I somewhat envy this approach, I don't know that I could live in such an uninhibited manner. My experience has taught me that the burden of a carefree life is always carried by someone else. At the end of life, someone will have to make the decisions I mentioned above. The person who has a plan and shares it with their loved ones tends to have a more peaceful death. The person who neglects this final responsibility often creates a more stressful grieving environment.

In business, like in life, a well-thought-through plan helps maintain the calm. In the book *The Functions of the Executive,* Chester Barnard wrote, "Organizations are held together by information, not by ownership or command." The best businesses not only have a plan, but also clearly communicate the plan.

Have a plan and make it known. Any business that cannot clearly articulate the reason for their existence, the values with which they will conduct their business, and their objective is like a rudderless ship on the open seas. So true is the adage, "If you don't know where you are going, any road will get you there." Businesses, both profit and non-profit, will do themselves a favor if they can succinctly define who, what, and why they exist. Even the best business leaders have difficulty publicly conveying their company's mission, vision, and values.

Granted, there are plenty of successful businesses in which mission, vision, and values are not widely known. However, the ones that tend to have long-term, sustainable growth are those that have a plan. Few businesses stumble into greatness. In the book, *Good to Great*, Jim Collins writes, "One of the dominant themes from our research is that breakthrough results come about by a series of good decisions, diligently executed and accumulated one on top of another."

Additionally, there is a growing sentiment toward working for and doing business with companies that have a social conscience. People gravitate toward companies that have a mission, vision, and values that are similar to their own personal convictions. So the business grows and people feel good about their association with the business. It's a win-win proposition.

Whenever someone applies for work at our agency, I assume that they have a personal mission, whether written or unwritten, that aligns with our corporate mission. People are looking for careers where their personal values align with the company in which they seek employment.

Companies will be wise to show the correlation between the two. The closer the alignment the greater chance for a long-term work relationship.

What is your plan? Where do you want to go? What do you want to do? What do you want to add or remove from your life? One important element in answering these questions is to have a plan. Remember, in its early stage, the plan does not need to be perfect, or complete. Like writing a book, it will require many revisions prior to publication.

General George Patton said, "A good plan, violently executed now, is better than a perfect plan next week." Companies such as Lockheed Martin, Boeing, and Apple Computer constantly upgrade equipment as the technology improves. They do not wait until they have a perfect product to take it to market. In their industry, there is no such thing as a perfect product. This mindset keeps them striving to develop the next best thing. So make a plan knowing that it is not a perfect plan. The improvements will occur over time as the plan is adjusted to meet the demands of life.

In our effort to care for the dying person, hospice makes adjustments as needed. What may be working to control pain and agitation today may not work tomorrow. The equipment, personnel, and medicines that were initially prescribed may need to be adjusted as death approaches. Hospice care specializes in asking, "What is needed now?" It's not about next week, next month, or next year. It is all about right now.

So what is your most pressing concern today? What are you doing *today* in order to answer that question? Often we fail to have a plan or we fail to act on our plan. Either way, the days slip by, and so does the possibility of fulfilling the plan. What is one thing you can do today in working toward the plan? Remember, no decision is *a* decision.

Have you ever heard someone say that making a plan crimps their artistic expression? Then there is the person who feels that planning is unspiritual, too confining to their free-spirited ideals. The only problem with this thinking is that the rest of us are left to work overtime in an attempt to make up for this lack of a plan. Show me someone who fails to make and execute a plan and I will show you a coworker, spouse, or friend who has to work overtime in order to make up for this failure. Take an honest assessment of how you live life and see if you are causing unnecessary stress for others. Better yet, ask those around you. If so, make a plan.

Too often, a dying person's refusal to engage in making and articulating an exit plan causes unnecessary stress for those left behind. Why should your loved ones be left with the task of making your final arrangements, disposing of your property, and cleaning out your garage?

I have had several conversations with grieving spouses, some who confess, with a degree of embarrassment, that they don't know what they are going to do with all their loved one's belongings. They should be focusing on the dying person, yet their minds are cluttered with what to do with their loved one's stuff. I admire all the people I visit, but I especially admire those who, prior to their death, have a plan. They sell the antique car, dispose of their tools, and clean out the shed. Why should I leave a mess behind for someone else to clean up? The dying person teaches me that having a plan helps keep the calm, for both them and their loved ones. So, what are you waiting on? This is the first day of the rest of your life. Make some movement toward your plan. Pick up the instrument, interview someone in your field, take pen to paper and sketch out an outline. It does not need to be perfect, but it does need to be practiced.

Make a Choice

Sometimes staying calm is as simple as making a choice. Sounds too easy to be true, doesn't it? But let me explain. Occasionally I find myself in situations where emotions are raw and human interaction intense. Studies show that the death of a loved one is one of the most stressful times in a person's life. And there are times when the family's grief is so palatable that it washes over me. My first inclination is to join in the mourning; however, in that moment I make a choice that I will remain sensitive to the needs, but focused on the task. I cannot own everyone's grief and expect to remain in this field long term. In other words, I make the choice to remain calm.

I imagine this is what emergency first responders do when coming upon a critical situation. They must choose to remain calm, even when everyone else is frantic. It is amazing listening to recordings of 911 call centers. The dispatcher calmly talks the caller through some harrowing situations. How do they do this? They make a choice to stay calm. They understand that the best way to deliver the necessary help is by remaining calm.

Why does it seem that the calmest parents are those who have ten children, while the most nervous parents are those who have one? Perhaps the parents with ten children have come to understand that they cannot personally keep all ten children safe from all of life's dangers. They have also learned to rely upon the older children to help care for their younger siblings. They simple have to make a choice that they cannot be everything to all ten children. They make a choice to acknowledge their limitations. On the other hand, parents of one child do their very best to protect their child from every and all danger, real and imaginary. They attempt to control the environment in which their child lives so that the child will only experience success. These parents also make a choice. They choose to control as much of life as is possible. The only problem with this thinking is, there is really little control any of us have in the truly important things of life.

Recently I sat with Ruth, an elderly woman whose husband, Bob, had died earlier in the month. They had been married for over fifty years. They shared mutual love and respect. She reminisced how her husband was always the calm one in the relationship, even when faced with a daunting challenge. She, on the other hand, was the worrier. It was evident that she was missing his calming voice and presence. I had the privilege to meet him two weeks before his death.

I suggested to Ruth that each day she take her worrisome thoughts, consider each one, and then place them into an imaginary bucket. After a few minutes, place the imaginary bucket to the side and enjoy the rest of the day. I did not suggest that she not worry; rather, I suggested that she take the time to worry and then take time not to worry. She looked at me and said, "I'll give it a try."

Whether or not she followed my advice is unknown. What I do know is that less than two months after her husband's death, she, too, unexpectedly died. When I heard of Ruth's death, I immediately thought of the words to the song, "Midnight Train to Georgia" by Gladys Knight & The Pips: "I'd rather live in his world than be without him in mine."

Life is full of choices. We make choices with our time, emotions, resources, and relationships. Even people who claim to hate making choices are faced with making choices. The most sedentary person makes a choice of non-movement. At the end of my life, I may make excuses about why I did or didn't do something, but the fact remains, it was my life to live.

My experience has taught me that people have more regrets over things they did not do than what they did. I have a quote on my desk that reads, "I would rather die with failures than die with potential." Each day we make a choice as to how we will live our life. We choose the thoughts we ponder, the attitudes we hold, and the actions we take. The choice is ours.

Some Final Thoughts on Staying Calm

Our youngest child, Jonathan, was in his final week of kindergarten when he decided to take my little pocket knife to school. While on the bus, he showed several classmates the knife. This was in the early days of the "Zero Tolerance Rule." If you were caught with a weapon, then it meant automatic expulsion.

I received a call from the school principal stating that she needed me to come to school in order to pick up Jonathan. My wife was unavailable because she was a student-teacher in her final semester. My mind was racing as I left work and drove to his school. Would Jonathan be expelled from kindergarten?

As I arrived at the kindergarten building, I remembered that this was the day for the end-of-the-year musical, *A Day at the Circus*. It was a circus-themed musical where each classroom dressed up in different animal costumes. The principal had a major role in the musical as master of ceremonies. She greeted the families and introduced each class song. Did I mention that she was dressed as a clown, red nose and all?

Once at the kindergarten building I was ushered into the principal's office and asked to wait for her arrival. She was in the gymnasium going over the pre-performance rehearsal. Jonathan looked at me, knowing that he was in trouble. Neither he nor I knew the extent of the consequences. Nor could we have imagined what was soon to be the most memorable part of this whole experience.

The principal walked into her office, fully dressed in her costume—red nose, face paint, and colored wig. She preceded to, in a very somber voice, speak of the seriousness of our son's actions, possible expulsion, and school board involvement. While I was cognizant of the possible punishment, I was consumed by the principal's red nose staring straight at me as she lectured both my son and me. It took every ounce of energy to refrain from busting out in laughter at this ridiculous sight.

I am thankful that Jonathan was not expelled from kindergarten, though he was suspended for three days, including the musical. While the pocket knife belonged to me, I did not feel complete ownership in my son's curiosity and behavior. Rather, my wife and I reminded him of the need to follow school rules.

So much of what happens in life is out of our control. But what is in our control is how we respond. Staying calm is a choice that we all make, or not. Do you really want to stay calm? It may require educating yourself in calming techniques. It may require being accountable to others, and it certainly may take an examining of your values and priorities. But a calmer you is possible.

This is not to say that we should always be calm. May I suggest that, when the house is on fire, you ditch the calm demeanor and get everyone out of the house? But at the same time, your house doesn't catch on fire every day, so why act as though it does? There is a time for high emotion, but that time should not come around daily. If it does, then it may be time to make a choice.

Questions

1. Do you find it difficult to ask for and/or accept help? If so, why?
2. What important insight have you learned about staying calm by reading this chapter?
3. Have you known someone who died without having made known their final wishes? How did this effect their loved ones' grieving process?
4. Do you make time for rest? Do you find it more difficult to slow down your body or your thoughts?
5. What reality—a relationship, career fit, or physical limitation—are you failing to acknowledge? How is this affecting you?

Chapter Three: Stay Humble

Living will humble you, and if living doesn't, dying surely will. My work as a hospice chaplain involves meeting people when they are at their most vulnerable, when the hope of recovery is diminished and their physical strength depleted. Dying teaches us something that living never can. The lessons are as varied as the students under its tutelage. Even in dying, a single day is never wasted.

The dying have taught me to be humble. Humble to walk with them in their final hours, and humble to consider my own journey's destination. The dying remind us of the importance of holding our loved ones tight and this world loose. They teach us that all we accomplish, accumulate, or aspire to be will remain behind once we draw our last breath.

But what does it really mean to be humble? Humble people are approachable, appreciative, and accepting of others. They are quick to forgive, slow to condemn, and timely in both word and action. They understand that they are not the center of the universe. Humble people acknowledge that there is always someone with a greater challenge. On more than one occasion, I have had a dying person look at me and say, "Others have it worse than me." Can you image saying that upon your deathbed?

Humble people have the best seat in life. They view everything and everyone from a vantage point that few of us enjoy. The proud person, on the other hand, has the worst seat in life. They see very little of what is truly happening around them. While they think that they have the best view, those around them know how blind they really are.

Several years ago, I visited Marlene, a woman in her seventies. She had recently moved into a nursing facility and was adjusting to her new surroundings. She had a private room and was allowed to bring in her own furnishings. What was remarkable about Marlene was her exquisite taste for fashion. Her room held a few pieces of her personal furniture, including a white chair and matching love seat along with accenting wall hangings and lamps. Marlene was always dressed in a nice outfit and her hair and makeup were freshly done.

While she had a terminal diagnosis, she maintained a well-put-together personal appearance. Marlene was always pleasant, engaging in conversation and welcoming of my visits. The only exceptions to this was on the days that the disease was getting the best of her. On those days, I simply respected her privacy and offered a silent prayer as I continued down the hallway.

One bright, sunny, Midwestern autumn day, I stopped to see Marlene, and, as was often the case, she was gazing out of her window. I accepted her invitation to sit and chat about whatever was on her mind. Early in the conversation, she pointed to one of several trees that landscaped the outside of the building. She asked me to look at one brilliant, colorful leaf among the thousands that were in their fall foliage.

Marlene asked if I would walk outside and get that leaf for her. I must admit, I could not distinguish which particular leaf she was referencing. After all, all the leaves were changing colors. But to Marlene, one stood out among the thousands.

Prior to walking outside to retrieve that leaf, I had the correct tree and I knew what side of the tree the leaf was on, but beyond that, I was in need of her direction. So I stood by the tree and began to point at different branches. Patiently, Marlene sat inside and signaled when I was getting close to the leaf. Finally, after a moment signaling back and forth, I had the correct leaf. So I gently pulled it from the branch and brought it to Marlene.

She was delighted to have that most distinguished leaf in her possession and thanked me for my effort. As I went on with my day, I reflected upon my visit with Marlene and what she taught me. While I looked out her window and saw trees, she looked out that same window and saw one leaf among the thousands. The dying person, the humble person, sees what the rest of us do not. We, too, can see what they see, if we simply take the time to learn.

Stay

In May of 1999, my father was diagnosed with mesothelioma, a form of lung cancer attributed to asbestos exposure. My father, having worked in the building trades for over twenty years, was affected by the material. At the time of my father's diagnosis, the treatments were in the early experimental stage. Few options were available, and even those offered no promise of a cure. My dad's perspective at that point was that if he could not be cured himself, perhaps his involvement in an experimental trial might help the next person. Here he was dying, but willing to participate in research that might help someone else. We truly finish life the way we have lived life.

At the time, my flexible work schedule allowed me the opportunity to drive my dad to treatment for his weekly appointments at the University of Chicago Hospital, where he received either the medicine or a placebo. (We were never told which of the two he received, and really it didn't matter, because the drug was not going to change his prognosis.) While the car ride was visibly painful for my dad, he continued to soldier on.

The most memorable car ride was one of our last ones to the hospital. It was wintertime when he began his treatments and we would often be driving home from the hospital as rush hour was beginning to build. This particular day was cold, overcast, and dreary. Commuters were slowly moving along the expressway, away from downtown and toward their homes. As we moved in procession along with the other cars, I looked over in the next lane and noticed a man in his mid-thirties driving his vehicle. The man was alone. It looked like the day's labor had gotten the best of him. He was wearing a tattered fleece jacket and driving an older model car. The car had several dents in it and the rear window was broken and partially open. Not a good situation on such a cold, damp day.

As my father and I drove just behind him in the next lane, I made a comment about what a tough life that guy is living. Without skipping a beat, my father said, "That used to be me." In that moment, I saw my father for who he really was. He was a hard-working, humble man who faced his challenges with determination and patience. He celebrated the good times and understood the priorities of family, faith, country, and community. (It is upon his generation's shoulders that ours now stands.)

My father's comment that afternoon remains with me these many years later. I never thought of my dad as the working poor, though he was in those early years of raising a family. The lasting impact of my father's comment remains due to his willingness to identify himself not with others' successes, but with their hardships. He was dying and he was humble. It was in his humility that he taught me life's most valuable lessons. So too with us, our children learn more from us when, in humility, we speak from a position of weakness rather than strength.

I realize that this is counter-intuitive for most of us. However, take a moment and consider the values and faith you hold. Did you come to embrace your values and faith from a position of pride or from a posture of humility? We listen best when we are ready to learn.

The challenges of a dying person are manifold. Not only do they face a myriad of physical, emotional, and relational changes, but they become increasingly more dependent upon others, including family members, close friends, and health care providers. Yet there are many similarities that dying people experience. This is one reason why hospice care is so timely with the delivery of equipment, medicine, and trained personnel. This is all we do. We see it every day and know what signs and symptoms to look for.

Humble People Accept Help

One of the challenges we as hospice providers are faced with is helping the dying person and their family understand that they will need help. Accepting help from others is especially difficult for those people who have always lived independent, self-reliant lives. They are challenged by the very thought of accepting help. The actual acceptance of the help is still another mental and emotional hurdle. Regardless of one's ability when healthy, when we are sick and dying the need for assistance is without question.

The sooner someone is willing to humbly accept help, the better for everyone involved. If an elderly husband refuses to allow our CNA to provide for his basic hygiene needs, and instead insists that his elderly wife provide this care, there is greater risk to him and to his wife. If a son is reluctant to give his parent the prescribed morphine due to his bias against such pain-killing medicine, his parent may suffer needlessly. If a family member declines chaplain support for their loved one because the family member, not the dying person, has an issue with organized religion, then the dying person may be denied an opportunity for inner peace.

From our vantage point, too many patients and their families experience unnecessary stress simply because they are unwilling to humbly accept the available support. On the other hand, the person who recognizes and welcomes interdependence tends to navigate this time with greater ease. Our own pride can be the biggest obstacle to experiencing a better quality of life.

In the workplace, accepting help is linked to collaboration, interdependence, and cooperation. You might be surprised how much healthier your work environment could be if success and failure were shared. Too often, upper management receives a greater share of the credit, or the blame. Often, personal ego stymies workplace interdependence. Seldom does a company's position in the market rise and fall on any one person. It really takes a team effort.

In the book, *Extreme Ownership: How U.S. Navy SEALs Lead and Win*, the authors write, "Everyone has an ego. Ego drives the most successful people in life—in the SEAL Teams, in the military, in the business world. They want to win, to be the best. That is good. But when ego clouds our judgment and prevents us from seeing the world as it is, then ego becomes destructive. When personal agendas become more important than the team and the overarching mission's success, performance suffers and failure ensues. Many of the disruptive issues that arise within any team can be attributed directly to a problem with ego" (100).

Humility can foster an attitude of cooperation with other companies. Does your company ever network with other businesses for the purpose of product innovation or addressing environmental concerns? When is the last time your company partnered with other local companies in order to address regional crime, poverty, and other social ills?

It takes humility to see other businesses not as adversaries, but as agents of accountability. I knew a CEO who made it his personal mission to speak ill of any competitors. He constantly maligned other agencies' practices. What he did not realize was that his obsession caused others to look at him in a less favorable light. Perhaps a little more professional humility would have elevated him in the eyes of others. We would do ourselves a favor if we would stop worrying about every other business and start minding our own.

Interdependence could mean being good stewards of the work environment, as well as taking the lead in protecting the population and natural resources. Remember what the dying teach us: We give it all back when we breathe our last. Nothing goes with us. Others will either enjoy the fruits of our labor or have to deal with the weeds that we have allowed to grow. In business, as in life, others will either speak well or ill of our efforts.

In relationships, interdependence is critical. The old adage, "In marriage, if one of you is not needed, then there is no marriage," is so true. In a family, if one member cannot discover what they bring to the family, the disconnect begins. Everyone needs to feel as though they have a role. Even the youngest child in a family must feel some sense of purpose. What contributing role do they have in the family? If mom or dad do everything to keep the home clean, connected, and cohesive, then the other members of the family begin to question their purpose. And the same goes for organizations. The pastor or school principal who find themselves doing everything in order to keep the organization moving in the right direction is doing too much. If that is you in your workplace or organization, then change must occur, and the first change must be with you. Either you are doing too much because of your own control issues, your unwillingness to mentor others, or your disconnect from the members of your family, congregation, or staff. No one was meant to travel this journey we call life alone. Early recorded history writes, *"It is not good for you to be alone, I will make you a companion."*

So when considering your life, with whom are you interdependent? Not dependent—but interdependent. Is that a small or large circle? How can you enlarge that circle in the next week, month, and year? What holds you back from enlarging this circle? Is it a lack of trust in people, or a lack of connections? Decide today to learn the lesson that all dying people learn—that is, the lesson of interdependence.

Humble People Are Real

Humble people are authentic people. People recognize a phony. You may have a good poker face, but as Pastor Pete taught me, the spirit never lies.

Pastor Pete was my coworker for over twelve years. Although he was twenty-five years my senior, we developed a good friendship. Often, we would confide in each other about workplace challenges. We also shared stories of the wonderful people we served.

Pastor Pete was a kind, loving, southern gentleman. His first day at hospice was delayed by three months due to emergency open-heart surgery. Throughout Pete's tenure at hospice, he faced mounting medical problems. At least twice a year he was in the hospital having surgery or receiving treatment for chronic illness. But through it all, Pete maintained a humility and a faith that God was with him.

While Pete was truly a gentleman, he held to a certain set of convictions, and no convincing was going to change his mind. Occasionally, Pete would find himself at odds with someone else's values. Often, he did not realize that the other person felt that way until our director called Pete into the office and talked to him about something he had said. On more than one occasion, Pete would look me up after one of these meetings and share his thoughts. It was never Pete's intention to offend anyone. He loved people and always had their best interest in mind.

Pastor Pete often said, "The spirit bears witness to the spirit." He meant that you can detect how someone feels about you by paying attention to what some may call "the spirit, instinct, energy, or inner compass." For Pete, this was the true test. Facial expressions, body language, even polygraph tests do not tell the full story. The spirit does not lie.

In any relationship, whether business, dating, or with neighbors, pay attention to your inner voice. If you are married, listen to your spouse. He or she may have a particular feeling about a potential business partner or deal. A wife, while she may not have a business background, is still your most trusted voice.

The landscape of human history is littered with the carnage of people who did not listen to the voice of a trusted friend or family member. About the most talked about death in human history, Jesus of Nazareth, it is written that the wife of Pontius Pilate warned her husband to have nothing to do with Jesus. Did he listen to his wife?

Do you want to have better relationships? Then pay closer attention to your inner voice. Do you want to be a better parent, spouse, or boss? Then listen. Listen not only to what is being said, but more importantly, to what is being sensed.

Much like my work, discovering and listening to this inner voice is as much an art form as it is a science. I ascribe to a particular set of personal and professional standards. Whether interacting with our staff or the family of the dying, my behavior must remain above reproach.

My agency has a set of policies that are expectations for employment. In addition, my ecclesiastical endorsement has a set of professional standards for those of us who are ordained. I am accountable to these ascribed standards. These standards, along with appropriate bedside manners, are the "science" of my work. The "art" form is understanding what is needed at that moment when I am at the bedside. Sometimes this is referred to as the "soft skills" in relating to others. While I may visit the same person numerous times, I never assume that the person is in exact same frame of mind or physical condition as my last visit. I approach each visit as unique, one of a kind, because I am aware of just how fast life can change in a short period of time. I approach each visit with an open mind, being sensitive to the subtle clues in their voice inflection, body posture, and tolerance level. These clues help frame each visit. The art form also includes those nuances of personal interaction and following your instinct. What takes place during a particular visit may not translate outside that moment in time; however, in that moment, it is the absolute best thing for the person. The visit is not about me, it is about them.

The first time I called Sam to offer a home visit, he asked me a question. He asked if I would give the eulogy at his funeral. It's not unusual to be asked to officiate at a funeral, but people often wait until after they have met me. Not Sam, he was direct and needed to get this settled. I agreed under one condition: we meet and then he could decide if he still wanted me to be involved. He agreed.

During my initial visit to his home, he told me about his life, family, and some of the challenges he faced. He reflected upon his thirty-five-year career as a grocery store manager. Immediately we had a connection. I, too, had worked in the same industry for two years just out of high school. I had an appreciation for the pressures under which he had worked. He also talked about a number of other concerns that he wanted addressed prior to his death. He diligently set about getting each one either started or completed. His concerns included major exterior home repairs and indoor electrical work. Did I mention that Sam was dying? Here, in the middle of one of the most stressful times in a family's life, he was scheduling contractors out to his house. It was a sight to behold. Building materials were stacked up in the driveway waiting to be used. All the while, Sam emphasized how blessed he felt. His father had died when he was nine years old and recently his younger brother had unexpectedly died. Sam was determined to die well.

During my second visit to see Sam and his wife, Marge, I experienced a conversation unlike any I have ever had as a chaplain. Sam's physical strength was visibly deteriorating, he had numerous home projects in motion, and he decided that he wanted a Doberman puppy. That's right, Sam wanted a puppy pincher. Talk about chaos.

As we sat at the kitchen table, Marge was constantly getting up and redirecting the rambunctious pup. Marge's stress was visible and at a dangerous level. At this pace, she would be in the hospital with her own health-related issues.

The science of chaplaincy—that is, appropriate bedside manner—would allow for conversation that might lead Sam to see that having a pup may not be the best decision at this time. However, on this occasion, having known a little bit about Sam's direct nature, I spoke to him in a direct manner, more direct than I have ever spoken to anyone else under hospice care. I said, "Sam, you need to get rid of this dog. If you don't, it will not end well for you or Marge."

While Sam did not like what I had to say—he became quiet and visibly irritated—he understood that my goal was to help him reach his goal of finishing well. At the current pace, neither he nor Marge were going to finish well.

This is the art form that I am referencing. It may not translate under any other setting, but in that moment in time, with those individuals, and with the backdrop of knowledge that I had, it worked. Not for my benefit, but for Sam's.

Two weeks later, I made my final visit when Sam was moments away from death. Did he finish well? Yes, Sam got his wish. Was Marge at peace? Yes. Did the pup remain in the house? No. Something had to give, and Sam accepted the fact that his wife's health was paramount to his desire for a puppy. The following week we gathered in honor of Sam's life, love, and legacy. I offered the eulogy in which I credited Sam with finishing well.

People will trust you, not because of the smile on your face or you carefully crafted words, but because of the spirit you project. Sam was willing to accept my help because he knew deep in his spirit that I was there to help. I knew deep in my spirit that Sam was sincere in wanting to finish well, and that made all the difference.

Humble People Are Teachable People

An old-timer once told me, "A short pencil is better than a long memory." I've never forgotten his statement and often hear myself telling others the same. It reminds me that we can learn from anyone, if we are willing.

Hall of Fame Coach John Wooden wrote, "When we stop learning, we stop living. Every day we have the opportunity to learn." What lessons do the dying teach us? First and foremost, they teach us how to finish life, and how to finish well.

There are occasions when family members are confused as to why their loved one is lingering for so long. They see no value in a prolonged death, and for a long time, neither did I.[But I have learned that every day has value, especially the difficult ones. No experience is ever wasted, if we are willing to learn from it, and the final dying days have much to teach all of us.]

When you spend your career, as I have, working with families, you quickly discover that every family has dysfunction, some more than others. I consider dysfunction a part of our flawed human nature. However one wants to define it, we are imperfect beings. For example, not every parent is a good parent. In fact, some are neglectful, and others are downright abusive. At the end of their life, this reality is heightened. It is difficult to hear stories of how this now-adult child was treated by their parent. What is more, the hope of any change quickly fades away as their parent moves closer to death. Some are able to momentarily push these feelings aside, while others still live under the cloud of hurt. To these individuals, I say, learn the lesson of how not to live.

At the same time, not every son or daughter is a good example of how to treat a parent. Some treated their parents with disrespect and dishonor. They made life difficult for their parents. Whenever they called their parents, it was usually when they were in trouble and needed someone to bail them out.

On one occasion, our nurse called me and asked if I would contact a certain family due to what the nursed termed "stressful spiritual issues." I placed the call and followed up with a home visit. What I quickly discovered was that there was no spiritual issue. This was simply a smoke screen for the real issue. As I spoke with the son, Aaron, who was his mother's primary care person, I discovered that the real issue was money. There was another son, Andrew, who had borrowed $10,000 from their mother, Liz, many years prior and never repaid her. Now Liz was dying, and the reality that Andrew would pay her back was dying with her. Aaron was learning an important lesson about Andrew, and he resented the fact that Andrew had taken advantage of their mother for most of their life.

The dying teach us that long-standing, often forgotten issues are never really forgotten. We may forgive, but we never forget. Sibling rivalries, unless dealt with, remain sibling rivalries. A lack of forgiveness toward a family member, unless addressed, will remain. We may frame it as a spiritual issue or a personality difference, but an offended person is unyielding.

Family challenges can be multifaceted considering the fact that many of us come from families with stepchildren or half-siblings. We can feel an allegiance to certain family members and as a result, establish alliances within our own family. These alliances become clear when death is near, as death has a way of bringing unresolved issues to the surface.

Life will teach us if we are willing to learn. If life doesn't teach us, death certainly will. Experience really is the best teacher. As a parent, I have discovered that no amount of talking will affect our adult children as much as experience. We can point people in a good direction, we can even share our experiences, but most of us have to learn it for ourselves. We need to experience it before we finally learn the lesson. There are some who never learn the lesson, and that in itself is a lesson.

So what are you learning today? What lessons are being taught to you through the good times and the bad? Is our pride standing in the way? Do we resist learning because of resentment or lack of forgiveness?

On one occasion, I scheduled a visit with Donald, an elderly man who was still living in his home. I knew his son-in-law, Rick, from a previous work experience. When I arrived at the home, Donald was in bed, actively dying. His wife, Judy, was seated on the couch near him. She was unaware just how close Donald was to death. As we sat near Donald's bed, I could see that he was breathing his last breathes, so I asked Judy to come alongside him. She took his hand, and within a minute he was dead. This was a sacred moment. Only five minutes in the home and Donald died.

Fast forward two years, and now Judy is under our hospice care. One particular Saturday night I received a phone call from her son-in-law, Rick, who informed me that Judy had gathered the family around her and was requesting that I come see her. As I arrived at the house, Rick met me outside in order to tell me that Judy has said farewell to her family and is ready to die.

Upon entering the house, I saw Judy in the same place that Donald had been two years prior. In addition, numerous family members were gathered around her, some tearful. As I walked over to her, I noticed that Judy was awake, talking with her family. This is not what I expected. She looked at me and told me that she would like to have prayer and then die, just like Donald. She literally thought that once I said a prayer, she would die. After all, that is what happened with her husband.

My first response was to softly smile and tell her that her death was not going to be exactly like her husband's, even though that is what she wanted. Though I could not give Judy what she wanted, what I did offer her was the assurance that her time was coming soon, and, when God was ready, He would call her home. Home to be with Donald and her only daughter, Angie, who had also died unexpectedly that year.

Three days later, Judy's prayer was answered, as she gently finished her earthly life. Judy taught me and her extended family the importance of preparedness, acceptance, and trust. But she also learned the valuable lesson of acceptance, patience, and trust as she prepared for her journey home. We never stop learning. Life forces us to learn. Even on our deathbed, we are learning about ourselves, about others, and about our belief system.

I first heard about Roy from our nurse who had visited him earlier in the week. As we met for our weekly interdisciplinary team meeting, the nurse stated that Roy and his wife, Sandy, had a pig living in their house. From that moment, my curiosity was piqued. I had made hundreds, even thousands of home visits and had witnessed many unique and unusual sights. But a pig living in a house, this would be my first.

When I arrived at Roy's home, I was greeted by Sandy, who spoke of her appreciation for the hospice staff, acceptance of the prognosis, and of their support system. Following a few minutes of conversation, she led me through their house in order to meet Roy.

It's not unusual for me to visit people in their bedrooms. After all, this is where many of us spend time when we are ill. So as I made my way back to meet Roy I could see through the bedroom doorway that he was in bed. After I walked in and introduced myself, Roy invited me to have a seat next to his bed. As we began to talk, he introduced me to his pet. Sure enough, I looked over my left shoulder and there on the floor of their closet was a 300-pound black pig, softly snoring.

I have never seen anything like it before, or since. Looking back upon that visit, there are several remarkable memories, but one that remains is that there was not a distinct hog smell in the house. Having worked on a pig farm while in college, I still have a sensitivity to the smell of pig. I need not digress.

As we talked that morning, the thought of there being a large pig laying a few feet from me quickly faded. What I had assumed might be the focus of my visit had little bearing on our conversation. The pig was a part of the family. It was no big deal to Roy or Sandy; therefore, it was no big deal to me either. Because I was willing to follow Roy's lead as to the unusual house pet meant that I was able to show up and learn, rather than be distracted by something that didn't matter.

Staying teachable means being willing to learn from others. You may feel resentment toward a supervisor, teacher, or coach; however, you can learn from them. We learn from others not only what to do, but also what not to do.

Sometimes we assume that the wealthy and or highly educated have all the answers to life's challenges. I have discovered that some of the poorest, least educated people in our community have insight about life and love that few possess. I have met couples who have expressed such wisdom regarding love and commitment that they didn't learn from a textbook or inherit from affluent parents. Rather, they allowed life to teach them the value of family priorities.

Whether I pull up in front of a million-dollar home or a rusty, single-wide trailer, I never know what relationships are formed within or the lessons they can teach me, so I enter into their life's journey and remain teachable. I have learned some of the most extraordinary life lessons from some of the most ordinary people, including lessons on forgiveness, perspective, and love.

The Great Migration (1915-1960) involved the movement of approximately five million southern blacks to the northern and western United States. They moved to states such as Illinois, Michigan, Pennsylvania, California, and Oregon with the hope of a better life. I have had the distinct honor to meet many who were a part of this migration as either children or young adults. Now they are at the end of their life and receiving hospice care.

My first visit with Miss Mae, age ninety-three, was scheduled and confirmed with her adult daughter. Miss Mae lived in a senior living apartment complex. When I arrived at her building, she gave me access to her sixth-floor apartment. I knocked on her door, and she called for me to enter.

Miss Mae was seated in a chair in her little apartment. She was physically fragile, but mentally and spiritually vibrant. She spoke of her family, her work, and how she came from Mississippi during the Great Migration as a teenager. She acknowledged that life was difficult as a child in the South, but that her faith in God and the hope of a better life provided motivation. There was not a hint of bitterness or resentment in her voice.

As she recounted a few of her life experiences, I found myself searching for a way in which to identify with her. Other than our Christian faith, my life's journey had none of the markings as Miss Mae's.

As our visit was concluding, I asked Miss Mae if she would welcome prayer. She agreed. Before our prayer, I leaned in toward Miss Mae and told her that I was sorry for the prejudice and unacceptable treatment she had received during her lifetime. I asked that she would forgive me for all the ways in which she was discriminated against. I told her that I was sorry for the many unnecessary hardships she had faced. Without hesitation, she leaned in toward me, placed her fragile hands in mine, and told me that she held no bitterness in her heart. She spoke only of God's goodness and blessings. Together we gave thanks to God for His abiding presence and His promise to lead. She thanked me for my visit and bid me good-bye.

One week later, I visited Miss Mae for the second and last time. During this visit, there was no conversation. She was non-responsive and only hours from death. Later that night she made her final and great migration to a land she had longed to see, Beulah Land, as some of the faithful used to sing.

While her formal education was limited to grade school, I learned more from Miss Mae about faith and forgiveness than I had learned from all my seminary professors combined. Miss Mae taught me that even if I experience hardship, abuse, and injustice, these need not determine for me my outlook on life or of others, even those who may have caused me the pain. I learned about our nation's history, not from the pages of a book, but through the eyes of sojourner. She taught me that the pressures of life can either make us bitter or make us better. She chose the latter and that made all the difference.

Some Final Thoughts on Staying Humble

My primary professor in seminary, the late Dr. Robert Lowery, often said that the most important context when studying an ancient manuscript is the "context of humility." That is, we, the student, should approach our study with a humble attitude. We should refrain from projecting our own bias upon the text. Rather, we should allow the manuscript to speak for itself. His words have application in many areas of life.

How much of our lives do we live with a built-in bias? We form opinions about people, places, and problems, often with little understanding. How much different would our lives be if we viewed everyone, including ourselves, from a context of humility? That is, allowing the individual life (and culture) to speak for itself. What lessons could we learn from others and how might our lives be enriched if we put aside any bias? This requires humble self-awareness.

To be humble is a choice. It requires a willingness to put aside any pretense regarding our own station in life. It properly sets our life in the context of humanity as a whole. Perhaps this is what the authors of the

Declaration of Independence had in mind when they wrote, "We hold these truths to be self-evident, that all men are created equal, that they are endowed by their Creator with certain unalienable Rights..."

Humble people possess an ability to properly assess and evaluate their life within the context of the world in which they live. Humble people understand that their life is not any more or any less significant than the next person's. This certainly bears out to be true as we finish life. Death is the equalizer. Power, prestige, and position are incapable of negating this threshold.

I began this chapter by writing that life will humble you, and if life doesn't, then dying certainly will. Let us learn to be humble, for it is a learned trait. Let us remain, for a lifetime, under its tutelage, for it will certainly instruct us in our final course. Let us come to better understand the manifold benefits of a humble life, including self-awareness, gratitude, and peaceful coexistence. Humility is truly one of life's great virtues and the one that accompanies us on our final day. Let us, today, become better acquainted with its voice.

Questions

1. Name a time in life when you were humbled by either another person or a particular problem or hardship. How did you respond?
2. As a child, were the adults in your life good examples of demonstrating humility? Why or why not?
3. Do you tend to follow your instinct when dealing with people? Explain how this is expressed.
4. What is one of the most unusual situations you ever found yourself in? What did you learn about other people? What did you learn about yourself?
5. Have you ever known someone like Miss Mae, who in spite of their own personal life challenges, they maintained a grace toward others? How were they able to maintain that sense of humility?

Chapter Four: Stay True to Yourself

Recently, I was given a DNA ancestry identification kit. The purpose of the kit, of course, is to identify in which regions of the world your ancestors lived. It's quite remarkable if one simply considers the rapid advancement in scientific technology during the past generation. Then there is the human curiosity of discovering something about one's roots. I am assuming that my findings will identify Irish and Italian roots; after all, that's what our parents told us. However, if the results determine that I have ancestry in other parts of the world, then I will be left to imagine how the lineage all fits together. I am willing to accept the fact that, in my family history, there may be unusual personal stories. In fact, I would probably be disappointed if at least one unusual character didn't surface in a genealogical search. My wife Kim is of the opinion that it's probably best not to look too closely into one's family history, lest you discover a bit of history you would rather not know. She may have a point.

Our heritage, the values we are taught, life experiences, and genetics all have a part in forming who we are. Being true to ourselves does not mean that we are stagnant or stuck in our human development. Nor am I suggesting that we are unable to pivot from long-standing convictions or beliefs. The genius of the human species is that we are able to embrace or discard personal values. While I cannot change my heritage, I can choose which long-held cultural and family norms I will uphold, if any. This is being true to myself. My parents, siblings, friends, and others have all helped me develop into the person I am. However, I have not been solely influenced by any one person or event. My life, and yours, is the confluence of too many of life's occurrences to single out any one in particular.

Being true to yourself means just that, being true to yourself. While I honor family heritage and values, learn from life's experiences, and identify genetic markers, I am not bound by any one influence. I choose how these factors will affect my life. As a friend of mine once said, "It's your life, go live it." In that moment, that simple sentence had a profound, if I may say, prophetic impact upon me being true to myself. It wasn't that I was lacking in personal integrity. Rather, having spent years serving others, I began to lose sight of what I wanted and needed in my life. Our world does not lack for people who are willing to tell us how to live our lives. So be true to yourself and go live your life.

A coworker of mine, Fran, embodied staying true to yourself. Not long ago, I attended her memorial service. Fran was a remarkable nurse who was beloved by the families she served. She was kind, compassionate, knowledgeable, and competent.

During Fran's memorial service, Fran's daughter, Ashley, spoke of how her mother, for three years prior to her death, had lived in an assisted living facility due to the onset of dementia. During this time, Fran welcomed any new resident into the unit as well as sat with the dying. She sang the Christian hymns of faith she had learned as child. In spite of the negative cognitive impact, Fran finished her life as she had lived her life. She was true to herself.

In life, we can spend an exorbitant amount of time and energy trying to please others. This is especially true for those of us who serve in the public arena. We spend so much time thinking about what others think that we sometimes lose a part of ourselves.

Have you ever been in a job where you knew that your workplace persona was not who you truly were? It's as if you had to mentally and emotionally get into your workplace character. Once the workday was over, you transformed into the real you. But the key to a happy life is being true to yourself. What motivates you? What gives you energy? What does a good day involve? These are just a few questions to ask when clarifying who you are.

Stay Strong

Whenever we look back through history, the people most often admired are those who have stayed strong under the most dire circumstances. Dr. Martin Luther King Jr., Winston Churchill, Abraham Lincoln, and Joan of

Arc are just a few of the names that come to mind when we think of people who are held in high esteem.

What do these people have in common? Why do we remember them? Because they stayed true to themselves and their convictions even under the crucible of life's mounting pressure. Yet none of the aforementioned heroes knew for certain the depth of their strength and character. It wasn't until their lives were placed in such precarious situations that their mettle was made manifest. Strength and courage are only fully realized when they are fully tested.

Dying is one of the greatest tests we will ever face. Our body, mind, and emotions are hard pressed during this time, while the hope of physical recovery is diminished and the thought of separation from loved ones is heightened. This process takes courage. It takes courage and strength of character to finish our course. We never know how much courage we have until we begin to draw upon it. Courage is like a deep well whose depths are unknown: We draw upon it until either it is used up or the challenge is met.

Inner strength usually develops over the course of a lifetime. People who are strong willed—or stubborn, if you will—have developed this strength through facing life's challenges. In Tom Brokaw's book, *The Greatest Generation*, he speaks to this strength of character of those from this generation. I have had the honor of visiting many from this generation. What is common to most is their unwillingness to surrender to the ravages of sickness and disease. Consider their story: As children, they struggled through the Great Depression, and as young adults they rallied to the cause of a world war. After the war, they worked in the factories, built the roads, and transformed this country along with much of the industrial world. They worked hard and completed tasks—they got the job done, any job. For many of this generation, dying is another challenge they have to face, but they do not willingly succumb to the process because they do not know how to surrender.

Strength and courage is not reserved just for the older generation. I have witnessed hospice pediatric patients show similar courage, strength, and determination. From where do these children derive such strength? To me, this is a greater mystery. Many times, it is the dying child who helps his or her family accept the prognosis. These children are proof that age and experience are not the only indicators of courage and strength.

I first heard about Billy from our pediatric nurse. Prior to coming under our hospice, Billy was receiving treatment from a leading children's research hospital. However, the medicine was not eradicating the disease and so our hospice was asked to provide additional support.

Billy was a young teenager when he came under our care, and he remained with us for the duration of his young life. Our staff watched him grow through adolescence. There were several times when we thought he might not pull through some medical challenge. However, time after time, he surprised us and recovered.

It wasn't Billy's nature to simply sit idle and watch the disease take his life. He organized a toy drive in order to provide gifts for others at the children's hospital. What began as a simple toy drive developed into a community-wide effort that continues to provide thousands of toys each Christmas. In addition, Billy occasionally came into our office to volunteer. He wanted to fill his days with meaningful work. He was fun, focused, and fearless. He was a great example of courage and strength. Billy was someone who stayed strong. For Billy, staying strong wasn't a cliché or a theory; it truly defined him as a person. Did he experience times of discouragement and fear? Probably, but he did not let that hold him hostage. While I am saddened to write that Billy lost his battle with cancer, he won in life, in love, and in leaving a legacy. Few have done so much in so little time.

How do we know if we are courageous or cowardice? We don't—at least we don't know until we are tested.

Staying strong does not mean that you go out and look for trouble. In fact, at times it requires that you steer away from it. Consider the aeronautics industry. They build airplanes in order to sustain demanding conditions including wind shear, lightning, and snowstorms. However, just because airplanes are equipped to fly in such stressful conditions does not mean they look for these precarious situations. Flight routes are often adjusted in order to avoid these challenging elements. For another example, take a professional boxer. The strongest fighter in the ring is often the smartest, not the most violent. He knows when to assert his strength and when to conserve it. Knowing when to avoid an opponent's punch is as important as knowing when to throw one.

The dying person has a limited amount of strength for each day. He or she has to decide how to spend this limited resource. Through hospice, we encourage the person to decide where they want to spend their limited reservoir. If they want to spend it in conversation and time with children and grandchildren, then perhaps they should forego household chores. Occasionally a dying parent or spouse will spend their limited strength attempting to fulfill the same role they did when they were healthy. That is their choice, but they will quickly discover that they do not have the strength to do anything else.

Once a person understands that physical strength is a limited resource, they begin to use it more wisely. Most of us move through life seldom considering physical strength as being a limited resource. Like money, we think that our strength is limitless. But the truth is, we can build our strength and stamina, but we cannot bank it.

Acknowledge Your Weakness

Superman had kryptonite, Samson had Delilah, even Augustine, as described in his *Confessions*, wrestled with own moral weakness. The history of civilization is filled with individuals who succumbed to carnal, even evil, inclination, and by so doing changed the course of world history.

While the decisions that you and I make may not alter world history, they can certainly alter our family history. Acknowledging a weakness, be it moral, physical, emotional, or intellectual, can change the course of one's life. If you are aware of your weaknesses, which we all have, then you will certainly become aware of them when the pressures of death come in full measure. I have seen both the strength and weakness of humanity fully expressed.

When I first met Chuck, he was at home seated in his recliner, weak and emaciated, though calm and receptive to my visit. If you could image the stereotypical biker dude—big, gnarly, inked, wearing leather—then you have a pretty good visual of Chuck. Back in the day, he was quite the imposing figure. Now, having succumbed to his disease progression, he was a shell of himself. During my visit, he reflected upon his family, work history, and his affinity for Harley-Davidson motorcycles. He pointed to several pictures in the living room of him and the bikes he once owned. While reminiscing, he began to sob as he acknowledged that his life was quickly drawing to a close. Still in his forties, he was grieving a myriad of losses including family, friends, and many of the pleasures in life, riding being one of his favorites.

With his head bowed, he said through the tears, "I am not as tough as I always thought that I was. I never imagined how difficult dying would be. This is whipping my butt."

People who have lived with relatively few setbacks, like chronic illness, a career-ending accident, or family tragedy, are often surprised when confronted with an overwhelming loss. Like Chuck, we often imagine that we can handle any difficulty life may present. It isn't until we have lived within the limits of our ability, honestly assessed the available resources, and recognized our weaknesses that we fully come to terms with the situation. But acknowledging a personal or professional deficiency is not a sign of weakness; rather, it is a clear indicator of a person's healthy self-assessment.

I'll give you an example. Where would NASA exploration be had it refused to acknowledge the weaknesses in their process, design, and testing? It was NASA's acknowledgment of the design flaw in the space shuttle *Challenger* that allowed it to learn from their deficiencies, correct their design, and move on to further exploration. They did not quit after discovering faulty equipment and processes. Rather, they learned from their organizational weakness and doubled their efforts. Perhaps this was the best way to honor the life and memory of those lost on that fateful day.

Chuck was honestly reflecting upon his current situation, or as they say in German, Sitz im Leben (setting in life). He was feeling the full effects of what life is, not what he thought it was going to be. More importantly, he was reflecting upon how he actually felt in the moment. His feelings were consternation, grief, and discouragement. This emotional, intellectual, and physical response was somewhat foreign to him. In that moment, my role was one of reflective listener, empathetic sojourner, and encourager. I listened because that was what he needed. I empathized with his manifold losses because I cared. I encouraged because, as his journey continued, he would need courage to finish.

My second and final visit occurred days before Chuck's "very last ride." By then his reaction to the pending prognosis had changed. He was minimally responsive and fully engaged in the dying process. Both his and my responses were different from the previous visit. Words were few, because words were not needed. Now, quiet presence and prayer were all I offered.

The benefit of acknowledging one's weakness is applicable in all areas of life. The person doing the military reconnaissance, operating machinery, or sitting at the bedside has a clearer understanding of how efforts are working than the person in the war room or boardroom.

I have noticed how true this is in hospice work specifically. Hospice work really is teamwork. Each discipline has a defined role in providing the necessary care. Ninety-nine percent of the time staff stay within their field of expertise. The only time a problem surfaces is when a team member either abdicates their role or attempts to do another team member's job. When this occurs, the result is either resentment, frustration, or misunderstanding within the team.

Contrast this with the medical doctor who asks the CNA not only her opinion, but then follows through on her perspective. The reason being, the CNA, who is frequently in the home, has a better understanding of the pressing concerns. The doctor acknowledges his ignorance on the person's current condition, but uses his expertise to address the need. Refusing the input of other team members may cause the person needless suffering.

I have discovered that one of the most liberating sentences for me is, "I don't know." It is amazing how my stress level is reduced simply by acknowledging that I do not know something. Now, I unabashedly acknowledge whenever I do not know something. I have discovered that whenever I acknowledge my lack of knowledge, there is often someone nearby who possess the necessary know-how. It is in my confession of ignorance that another person can rise to the occasion and solve the problem. They accept ownership in finding a solution. This environment encourages collaboration and provides others the opportunity to use their talents and intellect. Without my acknowledgment, they might remain unengaged.

So when is the last time you asked for help? Do you readily admit when you do not know something? How much needless stress do you carry because you fail to acknowledge what you do not know?

Embrace Peculiarity

What do the television series *The Addams Family* and *The Munsters* have in common with your family and mine? Quite a bit. You see, on the one hand, like most typical families, they are simply trying to live out their lives. Similar to these characters, our families also have different personalities and idiosyncrasies. Maybe not as extreme, but the differences are recognizable. The advantage that these television family icons have over us is that they never think of themselves as being peculiar. They unapologetically embrace their uniqueness. It is their guests who the viewer begins to think of as strange.

I can unequivocally say, having had the opportunity to meet thousands of families, that we all have a little family peculiarity. From hoarders to hippies to homesteaders, I have met them all. The sooner we acknowledge and accept our diversity, the better.

Each person has his or her own unique personality and perspective. No two people see the world exactly the same. Like our fingerprint, we are truly one of a kind. How we process thoughts, feelings, languages, and relationships are unparalleled. Our differences are our strengths. We are each like a single thread woven into the tapestry of the world around us.

Every person's life brings something that adds to the overall beauty of creation. So let's celebrate our differences and acknowledge the genius in human design.

It is easier for someone to express their peculiarity in our current culture as compared to previous generations. Today, diversity is encouraged and celebrated. In fact, there is so much diversity, especially in the urban centers, that it is difficult to stand out among the crowd. Body piercings, tattoos, hairstyles, and clothing options are a few of the ways in which people express their uniqueness. The shock value of these style choices has worn off so that what was once rare has become commonplace. People may stop and look, but gawking at a strange-looking person does not occur as frequently as it once did. Besides, with the widespread availability of cable television, people have greater access to view and mimic unusual characteristics, so much so that cultural outliers are no longer only living in some coastal commune. Today, almost every family has at least one member who exhibits some form of personal expression.

Going a step further, expressing one's uniqueness is encouraged in our society. Not only is it accepted, but also it is taught in schools and the workplace. Most businesses require their staff to receive training in diversity, inclusion, and building cultural competence. Our world is getting smaller.

During my hospice visits, it is common for a family to try to explain a particular family arrangement. I attempt to quiet their concerns by accepting the situation as it is. After all, it's their life to live as they see fit. Unless there is an unhealthy, dangerous home environment, I simply accept people. As my father used to say, "It takes all kinds to make the world go round."

Recognize Personal Prejudice

Embracing diversity allows us to recognize and honor all different kinds of people and cultures. The intent is to accept all expressions of personal and familial diversity. Cultural sensitivity and cultural allegiance can, and should, co-exist. And yet, we all hold preferences or prejudices. We all have our favorite sports team, rock band, and author, and it can be difficult—if not impossible—to persuade us to another way of thinking.

I will give you an example from my own life. I seldom order pasta with red sauce from an Italian restaurant. The problem isn't with the restaurant; the problem is with me. You see, I grew up enjoying homemade sauce that my mother slow-cooked all day long. Now I can't order this meal at a restaurant because no one makes it like mom. I have a taste preference for our family recipe.

Failing to recognize prejudices, even harmless ones like my preference for my mother's red sauce, can create personal and professional challenges that are difficult to overcome.

Along the same lines, as a person nears the end of life, it is important to understand and honor their particular cultural practices, rather than embrace what might be our own personal prejudice against them. At hospice, we try to pay particular attention to these practices. In our assessments, we ask the person and their family if they have any particular cultural or religious traditions for the dying, and if they do, we honor these practices. This helps us ensure that we help the dying stay true to themselves.

However, there are rare occasions a staff member's personal preference about managing symptoms is in conflict with a person's medical, religious, or personal convictions. Even if our staff member has experienced a long history or success with managing others with this particular symptom, they must listen to the patient's and caregiver's concerns.

While my role on the hospice team does not involve the ordering or administering of medication, I have watched with curiosity a patient's and their family's acceptance or rejection of certain medicines. Central to this discussion is the use of morphine, a pain medication of the opiate family. It does not occur often, but there are times when the patient or caregiver sees the offer of morphine as taboo. It behooves our nurse to listen to and honor the concerns of the families we serve. Even if the nurse knows that a particular medicine will address the immediate need, they must set aside their knowledge, experience, and preferences in order to honor the family's concern. Often, given enough time, the family will accept the nurse's suggestion.

Whenever a person voices an objection to any of our services, including medicine, equipment, or personnel, it is incumbent upon our staff to honor that request. Recently I called Frank, an eighty-six-year-old man who was enrolled under our services. His daughter, Diane, answered the phone, at which time I introduced my role on the hospice team. She thanked me for the call but informed me that her dad was not a religious man and that he would not be interested in my visit. I reminded her of my availability and thanked her for the time.

Fast forward two months, and Frank was experiencing increased end-of-life symptoms. He mentioned to Diane that he was receptive to a chaplain visit. The following day, I visited Frank and Diane. While Frank acknowledged that he is not a religious man, he did reflect upon his service in the military, his forty-year work history at the local factory, his volunteer work at the community center, and that he and his late wife, Martha, raised eight children. As I sat there listening to Frank share part of his life story, I saw a man who spent his life serving others. He served his country, he served his company, he served his community, and he certainly served his family. As we concluded our visit, I remarked to Frank that he spent his entire life in the service of others. Neither Frank nor Diane had seen his life in that light. In those few moments together, I simply held up a frame that Frank and Diane could look through and see his life in a different way. While Frank was not a religious man—by his estimation, not mine—he was a man who made a difference in the world in which he lived. I reminded Frank and Diane of the words, "Whatever you do for the least of these you do as unto God." I thanked Frank for his service and for a life well lived. Later that month, Frank served his family one last time as he peacefully and willingly transitioned from this life to the next.

Experience has taught me that I will be where I need to be when I need to be there. I have learned that there is no benefit to me or others by attempting to force a visit because I, another team member, or a family member thinks that this is what the patient needs. Remember, the person sets the agenda. Time and again, after first rejecting a visit, I have watched a family member call the office or convey the request that the person is now welcoming of a chaplain visit. Being willing to set aside personal prejudice or preferences helps create an environment where something special can occur. Had I attempted to impose a visit upon Frank earlier than he was willing to accept, or misrepresented my role, Frank and Diane may not have been as receptive. By being true to myself, I am able to serve the greater good of others.

Be it the administration of medicine or the acceptance of a minister's visit, paramount to serving the needs of others is recognizing and respecting their wishes. Whenever I fail to recognize and confront my prejudice, I fail to honor another person's life. Maintaining heathy relationships requires me to confront all personal prejudice and to take an honest look at the actions and attitudes that frame my life.

The Lesson I Learned from a Beer Truck Driver

I have spent my entire career in some form of pastoral care ministry. During the past thirty years, I have served as either a congregational pastor or health care chaplain. Part of this work has involved counseling. While I have counseled many individuals and couples, I never feel adequate for the task. Neither do I derive much personal satisfaction. I do it because people ask me based upon their trust.

I met Joe, a retired beer truck driver, and his wife, Ann, when they attended one of our church services. I was young—in my mid-twenties, full of enthusiasm, yet inexperienced in most of the demands of pastoral ministry. Counseling was one of my least favorite responsibilities and the one for which I felt the least prepared. When Joe asked to meet with me in order to provide marriage counseling, I tried to refer him to a trained counselor. Joe would have none of it. He insisted than Ann and he meet with me.

Two things were apparent as we began to meet. First, Joe was in terrible physical shape. He had a "beer" gut that extended far beyond his waistline. He suffered from high blood pressure, heart disease, and numerous other physical maladies. He often smelled of beer, though he never appeared intoxicated. Joe was a medical mess. However, in spite of all of his challenges, he maintained a pleasant, somewhat jolly disposition. His greatest concern was Ann's mental and emotion health.

Second, Ann appeared to be in as bad of shape mentally and emotionally as Joe was physically. Ann appeared despondent, depressed, and emotionally disconnected. I had never met anyone who appeared so mentally and emotionally crushed. She remained quiet during our first meeting. It was obvious that she did not arrive at this physical and emotional state overnight. This condition had developed over many years. Compounding her plight was an estranged relationship with their adult daughter, Laurie.

Joe was at a loss. He loved Ann and wanted to help her get better. Why they chose me to help them remains a mystery these many years later. Yet, we embarked upon a journey that, in my mind, had little promise of success.

The church I served at that time had no formal office space, so we met weekly in the nursery. Joe and Ann would sit in the two rocking chairs and I would sit on a folding chair. Looking back, it's a wonder they ever continued counseling, given our makeshift accommodations. But, each week they would show up and we would work through a number of personal issues. Progress was slow, methodical, and painstaking. However, there was progress. Not as I defined progress, but as they defined it. I do not recall how many months we met, but I do remember the physical, emotional, and relational transformation that they experienced.

Without reservation, I can say that their transformation had little to do with my professional counseling training, of which I had little. It had much more to do with our willingness to be honest, transparent, and true to ourselves. I did not pretend to be something I was not; I did not pretend to be a marriage counselor with all the answers. Joe and Ann did not pretend to have a marriage that was something other than it was. Together, we had open, honest conversation and together we looked for solutions. Looking back, that made all the difference.

One memory I still hold, over twenty-five years later, is the physical transformation that occurred with Ann. Like a flower in springtime, Ann came alive. I could see it in her confidence, her attitude, and her engagement with Joe and others. I have seldom seen such transformation in anyone since. What was it that brought about the transformation? I believe her willingness to be herself, to be honest, and to share what was on her mind, even if Joe or others did not agree with it, brought about this change. Slowly she began to stay to true to herself.

Ann had spent her entire life internalizing her thoughts, preferences, and ideas. In her attempt to take care of others, she had lost sight of who she was. This memory of Ann still reminds me that it is difficult to be true to yourself when you forget who you are.

Within a few months of concluding my time with Joe and Ann, Kim and I accepted a ministry assignment in another state. Within the year, I received a handwritten letter from Ann. She wrote to inform me that Joe had recently died and that she was adjusting to life without her husband of more than fifty years. She also wrote that both she and Joe felt that our time together was of great personal benefit, and that Joe often spoke well of me. My experience with Joe and Ann taught me that the best way to help others is to be genuine and true to myself. I learned that people benefit the most when we put aside the facade of being something other than who we are. Joe and Ann walked away from our time visibly changed due to our willingness to being true to ourselves. I walked away from the experience with a greater appreciation of the counseling process, a process that was based solely on our being honest with one another.

An Accidental Encounter

I first met Eleanor by accident, literally. I was at a gas station when I heard the terrible screeching sound of skidding tires and crashing metal. As I looked toward the sound, I saw a car spinning through the intersection, having just hit another car. I momentarily looked around, hoping that a police car or fire truck was in the vicinity, but to no avail.

While I was not excited about the possibility of providing first aid, of which I had little knowledge, I was the nearest to the accident and felt compelled to at least make the attempt. As I made my way over to the driver's side of one of the vehicles, I glanced inside and saw an elderly woman attempting to pick herself up off the passenger's side floorboard. I opened the door and proceeded to help her back to the driver's seat. As soon as she was reseated, off in the distance, we heard a police siren. As instinct would have it, she began to reach back over her left shoulder in an attempt to retrieve her seatbelt. (The seatbelt law had recently been enacted and Eleanor was worried about receiving a seatbelt violation.)

Without thinking, I said to her, "It's a little late for that." With that, she slumped in her seat and began to assess the physical damage. She had sustained a bruised arm and a few lacerations, but beyond that, she was alive.

During those few moments of attempting to keep her calm until the paramedics arrived, Eleanor told me she lived in the apartments behind the gas station. I learned her first name and the complex where she lived. Later that week, as I recounted my experience to some friends who happened to live in the same building as Eleanor, they realized they knew her and arranged for me to visit her.

Eleanor and I developed a friendship, and I visited her every few weeks. It became apparent to me that Eleanor suffered from Parkinson's disease, which was rapidly limiting her physical mobility. Due to the progression of the disease and other maladies, Eleanor decided to move into the local nursing home. It was a difficult but necessary transition.

Just prior to relocating to another state, I visited Eleanor in the nursing home. Her physical decline was quite apparent, and knowing that we would not see each other again brought a sense of sadness. Prior to our final good-bye, she welcomed prayer.

What had begun as a guarded acquaintance with Eleanor had evolved into a genuine friendship due, in large part, to the fact that Eleanor and I were honest with each other. Neither placed expectations on the other. We simply accepted each other while being true to ourselves, and this made all the difference.

Our culture is obsessed with celebrities. We see it in film, music, politics, even religion. The masses clamor for someone whom they can idolize. We often make these celebrities out to be people they are not. They, on the other hand, bear some of the responsibility by projecting a false persona.

It isn't until their personal character traits are exposed that we come to better understand them as a person.

We value authentic people. Yet, how do you know someone is authentic? We do in a similar way to, say, a painting or old coin. Personal authenticity is proven when it is tested. Dying is one of the greatest personal tests we face. Our true character shines through when we face death. My premise—that we finish life the way we have lived life—is validated as we walk through the valley of the shadow of death.

Dust to Diamonds

People who are generous in life are generous in death. People who are funny, carefree, or appreciative in life are so in death.

The first time I visited Grant at his home, a FedEx delivery arrived as I pulled into his driveway. No sooner had I sat down in Grant's living room than he asked if I would like to view the video that had just arrived. Grant and his wife, Geri, appeared so excited at the video's content that I could not refuse. As it turned out, the video was the recording from a Japanese news station detailing Grant's decision to have some of his ashes made into a diamond. The news reporter and cameraman had, in recent weeks, flown to the United States and interviewed Grant and Geri regarding their final wishes.

During my visit, I discovered two people who had a wonderful sense of humor. Even though Grant was dying, he maintained his ability to laugh, even at himself.

Several months later, Grant died after being taken to the emergency room for another issue. Later on, the attending nurse related to Geri that just before he left Grant's room for the last time, Grant had told a joke that caused the nurse to laugh. Grant truly finished his life the way he had lived it, bringing levity and laughter to others.

I have met many people who were not funny, kind, or generous. Rather, they were described by family members as being grumpy, stingy, and mean-spirited. Unlike Scrooge, they did not experience a change of behavior prior to death. Like Grant, they were true to themselves.

Do you ever wonder what type of person you will be when it is your time to die? What type of person are you today? This is the type of person you will be when you are dying. We finish life the way we have lived life.

Harold was one of the meanest men I have ever met. He made life difficult for everyone who met him, including our staff. His adult children said that their father was even mean to them. Anyone who crossed his path was treated with disrespect and disdain. Yet, his wife, Eleanor, was one of the sweetest persons you could meet. Like Grant, Harold finished his life the way he had lived his life.

Both Grant and Harold died over a decade ago; however, whenever I drive past either of their houses, I reflect upon the impression that remains. One left a memory of merriment, while the other a memory of discontentment. Each man's legacy is etched in the minds of those who knew him.

So how we live today really does make a difference. In fact, how we live this day has a tremendous influence on how we will live on that final day. How we live today will also create the memories of what others will remember about us long after we are gone.

Some Final Thoughts on Staying True to Yourself

My mom is in the twilight of her life as she continues to face a myriad of mounting medical challenges. It goes without saying that watching the slow decline of a loved one is difficult. Like a beautiful flower fading before our eyes, my mom's strength and her will to live slowly wane. She speaks more often of her desire to go to heaven than revisit the days of yesteryear. While it is difficult to hear such words from our mother, my siblings and I have come to accept the reality of her gradual transition. In working at hospice for these many years, I've learned that there comes a time where a person's prayer changes from, "God heal my loved one and make them whole," to "God be with my loved one and take them home." I am currently watching that transition occur within members of my own family.

There are several remarkable qualities about my mother that I have often overlooked, or perhaps, under appreciated. However, under the crucible of my mom's physical pain and mental anguish, I have come to better understand her. First, her commitment to look her best through the use of cosmetics and grooming remains steadfast. Without exception, whenever I visit my mom, her makeup is applied and her hair has been combed. It may not look perfect, but she always makes the effort. There have been a number of days I wanted to tell her that she did not need to spend the energy on these activities; however, it helps her feel better, so I refrain from speaking about such.

Second, she has always held to a love for God that has inspired her to share that faith with others. Since my childhood, I can remember times that we would be out in a store or restaurant and my mom would share her Christian faith. Often, I would roll my eyes in embarrassment or slowly walk away knowing that mom was taking time to encourage others in their life's journey. Even today, she makes the effort to encourage the nursing home staff as she shares her love for God. I find it personally interesting, and a bit self-revealing, how her efforts to do such do not seem to bother me as they once did. My mom is being true to herself, even in the midst of her own life's struggles.

Finally, as a mom, she is being true to herself in her desire to spend time with family. As always, her greatest joy is seeing her children, grandchildren, and great grandchildren. Regardless of how sick she feels, the best medicine is time with loved ones. Watching my mother during these twilight years have given me a strong example of how to stay true to myself as I move through life.

Questions

1. Why do we find it difficult to stay true to ourselves?
2. Name a time in your life when you were not true to yourself. What was the outcome?
3. If the premise, "We finish life the way we have lived life," is true, how do you image that you will finish life?
4. List three positive character qualities that others have identified in you. Do you see how they came to this conclusion about you?

5. How do you respond to others who are "true to themselves" but do not share your personal convictions? Does someone in particular come to mind?

Conclusion

Albert Einstein once wrote, "The important thing is not to stop questioning. Curiosity has its own reason for existence. One cannot help but be in awe when he contemplates the mysteries of eternity, of life, of the marvelous structure of reality. It is enough if one tries merely to comprehend a little of this mystery each day." Each day provides a new mystery to be solved. We are all given the opportunity to learn. Discovery comes through our interaction with others. No one holds the key to all knowledge and understanding; it is a shared commodity. Many of life's maladies could be solved if we understood just how interdependent we are with one another. Yet, differing cultures continue to malign and marginalize others. These attitudes are often based in fear and mistrust.

In this book I have provided four essential character traits—pillars, if you will—that provide the support for building and maintaining healthy relationships. These traits, when properly applied, help create an environment where mutual respect can be expressed.

Regardless of the relationship—be it work, family, or international diplomacy—there is room for improvement. The ability to stay focused, stay calm, stay humble, and stay true to yourself can be applied to any relationship with almost immediate impact. As a global community, we have made great strides throughout the past century. Advancements in communication, assimilation, and honoring, not fearing, other cultural traditions has fostered healthier connections. And as individuals, we have the opportunity to determine what will one day be written about our time on earth. A little "staying" power may help write a better story—one that we, and our children, can all enjoy.

To conclude, I would like to share a final story. When our son Joel was a pre-teen, I was driving a group of his friends to the park when one of the boys asked the others, "What does your dad do?" One by one, each boy told the others about his father's work. I was quite curious how Joel was going to answer the question. Finally, after all the other boys responded, Joel said, "My dad holds people's hands as they die." While I am certain that the other boys were a little bit confused by his answer, I drove on with a deep sense of satisfaction knowing that our son thought of me as a person who helps others.

I had no intention of working at hospice for all these years. My plan was to spend a year in this field and then continue my work in congregational ministry. Yet, as I look back upon the many years spent helping people finish their lives, I cannot think of a more rewarding career. The trust and access to their end-of-life journeys that individuals and families have afforded me is unequal among the workforce. I guard their trust and pray that the telling of their stories will help each of us write a better story. One in which we all finish well. Here's to a life well lived.

Finally, I conclude the book with a poem that was recently read at one of our agency's team meetings. When I heard it, I thought that it captured the essence of what hospice staff members experience as we enter into the lives of those finishing theirs. While I am uncertain of the poem's author, I am certain that they have experienced the kind of profound and life-changing privilege of being a hospice care provider. To all who serve others in a similar capacity, I say, "Thank you."

The Entering: A Poem

We enter their lives, their homes
A time of such turmoil and sadness
And we witness to the most remarkable
People that ever were.

We enter their homes, their lives
And marvel and wonder at what we see
And are touched by their courage and their
Willingness to share.

We enter their lives, their homes
Hoping to make a difference in the time that is left
Yet knowing all the time that in reality,

Stay

They will make such a difference in our lives,
That we will never be the same.

We enter their homes, their lives
And try to imagine how it would be if things were reversed
And we would be opening up our lives to complete strangers on a
Journey that we did not choose to take.

The entering - a relevant time
When we offer ourselves and we connect.
When we are saddened but also privileged and somewhat in awe
That we are permitted to witness the human spirit at its finest.

Made in the USA
Lexington, KY
17 May 2019